LOST IN CHURCH

LOST
IN
CHURCH

JONATHAN R. CASH

w
WHITAKER
HOUSE

LOST IN CHURCH

For interviews and speaking engagements, contact Jonathan Cash at:
In the Sky Ministries
P. O. Box 15770
Chesapeake, Virginia 23328-5770
Phone: 757.546.3313
E-mail: intheskyministries@juno.com
Web site: www.theageoftheantichrist.com

ISBN: 0-88368-758-5
Printed in the United States of America
© 2002 by Jonathan Cash

Whitaker House
30 Hunt Valley Circle
New Kensington, PA 15068
Please visit our web site at www.whitakerhouse.com

Library of Congress Cataloging-in-Publication Data

Cash, Jonathan R., 1965–
    Lost in church / by Jonathan R. Cash.
        p. cm.
    ISBN 0-88368-758-5 (pbk. : alk. paper)
    1. Spiritual warfare. I. Title.
    BV4509.5 .C384 2002
    243—dc21
                                            2002005230

1 2 3 4 5 6 7 8 9 10 11 12 / 09 08 07 06 05 04 03 02

Dedication

This book is dedicated to people who refuse to live a life of spiritual mediocrity. To those who are willing to earnestly pursue God, withstand the temptations of the flesh, and live out their Christian beliefs at all cost, I salute you for your wholehearted dedication. Never give up or lose sight of the ultimate goal: Life with God.

Contents

Many are lost in church because they have never drenched their minds and spirits with the water of life, the Word of God. Knowing God is knowing His Word.

As Christians we are called to be *transformed* by Christ rather than *conformed* to the world. Repentance is key to salvation. True followers of Christ are "on fire" for Him.

Our faith is evidenced by our works. The pretension of religion is no substitute for the real thing. Hypocrisy impugns God's reputation.

A person cannot love God and ignore His commands concerning money. Christians put their money where their faith is.

To fear God means more than dreading His judgment or rebuke. It means to reverence Him, to be in awe of Him, to worship Him.

Like a small spark among a dry forest, gossip spreads rapidly and can quickly turn into a raging inferno. A believer allows the Holy Spirit to control every part of his life—including his ears and tongue!

One of the signs of a true Christian is the ability to forgive unconditionally. A life characterized and controlled by unforgiveness is a life void of God's healing power.

We can become so desensitized to sin that we no longer recognize it for what it is. But the Holy Spirit fills a Christian's heart and makes his conscience Spirit-sensitized, helping him to walk in the ways of the Lord.

False prophets are alive and well today in many denominations. Identifying false prophets is a Christian's spiritual responsibility. The Bible gives clear directions on how to tell the difference between false and faithful teachers.

The traditional family is under attack like never before. The enemy lusts for control over you and your spouse, but with God's help, you can send the devil packing with his tail between his legs.

Religious pride, one of Satan's most lethal weapons, is capable of destroying soul and spirit. But when the Spirit of God fills a person's heart, there is no room left for pride. God doesn't want you to base your faith on your church, pastor, denomination, or religious status, but rather on His Son.

This is the real-life story of one man who was lost in church—and didn't know it. Jesus continued to pursue him until he was found. The Good Shepherd is relentlessly seeking the millions upon millions of His lost sheep in church. He is not willing for even one to be lost.

Foreword

In 1948 an astonishing event occurred as the Jewish people gathered from around the world and reassembled as a nation. The world was further shocked when in 1967 they recaptured part of Jerusalem, the Holy City. Jesus Christ made it clear that when this happened, the time of the Gentiles—when God grafted in the Gentiles so as to bring *"many sons to glory"* (Heb. 2:10)—would soon come to an end.

The problem of ancient Israel was that they thought their power was in their rituals and traditions rather than in God. As the great apostle Paul warned in Romans 11, the Gentiles may fall prey to the same disaster.

In this book, Evangelist Jonathan Cash, who is also the meteorologist for one of the highest rated television morning shows in the country, gives a forecast for such a coming storm. Jonathan tells with astonishing simplicity yet profundity about a people, like ancient Israel, who are blessed with the greatest heritage ever afforded humans—a personal relationship with Yahweh, the God of Israel—yet blinded by the world around them to His pure light and eternal glory.

Sadly, millions of people from every Christian denomination fit this description. Many trust in church membership to get them to heaven, while others trust in religious traditions. Some believe they will make it to heaven because they are "good" people; they try to do the right thing, at least most of the time.

These false doctrines are sweeping the casual, lukewarm churchgoers to their spiritual deaths. And where are the preachers of righteousness? Many fear their congregations more than they do the God who created them. Jesus wants followers to worship Him in truth and spirit; yet what is truth, and where can it be found? What does

God think of the twenty-first-century church? What does God want from us on a real and practical basis? My friend Jonathan Cash seeks to answer these questions.

When the Lord looks down from His throne in heaven, what does He see? Does He see holiness and repentance, or does He see something different, a subtle but deadly seductive spirit? Does He see the church peering over its "righteous" shoulder at other's infidelities, or does He hear the sincere cry, "Forgive me, Lord, for I'm a sinner"?

This book will change your life and direct you to the Author of Life, Jesus Christ of Nazareth, who yearns for your heart, soul, and mind—your very being. Just as a husband wants total devotion from his wife, Jesus wants a love relationship with you that is pure and unspoiled by worldly ways.

Are you ready to get real with God? Are you prepared to do some serious business with Him? It's the kind of business that will cost you everything, yet it's free to those who earnestly seek Him.

Martin Luther nailed ninety-five theses on the door of Wittenberg. Jonathan Cash, in this strikingly honest appraisal of the Christian church, hammers in one more: The Christianity of many around the world is not the Christianity of the Bible.

Lost in Church is a long overdue, genuine assessment of today's church. In a penetrating and provocative way, Jonathan Cash has spoken the unspoken truth we are all privately aware of: Building church facilities, packing pews, or boosting budgets are not substitutes for real Christianity. God is still seeking the lost, both in the world and in the church. Have you been found?

—Dr. Rick Amato
"The Preacher Dude"

Introduction

We live in a lost world, a world more frightening than anything Sir Arthur Conan Doyle could have imagined. Its fearsomeness lies not in prehistoric monsters, but in inhabitants who have turned away from their Creator and rejected the only Redeemer who could rescue them from their spiritual sickness. Disconnected from the God of grace, human beings live in disgrace, choosing to become their own gods. Burdened by their sins, they seek relief from the consequences of their actions but continue to do the very things that enslave them.

The prayer of Augustine, "Thou hast made us, O Lord, for Thyself, and our souls are restless until they find their rest in Thee," has been silenced by the winds of change: a change to more liberal theology, less emphasis on the Bible, and more reliance on individual experience as a way to reach God. Yet the restlessness Augustine spoke of infects their souls, leaving them with an insatiable quest to "find themselves." The search for self often leads to a religious experience in which the God of the Bible is thought to be nothing more than a whisper in the wind, a voice calling in a desert, or an opinion that can be easily ignored.

Alienated from God and His laws of living, they live their lives the way they want, unashamed of their double-mindedness and lack of faith. Like people who have deliberately spread the AIDS virus, they justify their search for self-satisfaction with rationalizations such as, "It's my body. I can do with it as I please." They are disconnected from God and others. Instead of truly loving people, they use them as objects for their satisfaction, tools for their self-fulfillment. God's will is replaced with

the will to pleasure self: "If it feels good, do it." Morality is lost in a sea of relativism, and as Paul said, *"The whole creation groans"* (Rom. 8:22 NKJV).

Can you hear the groaning of our lost world? Listen to the cries of young girls with unwanted pregnancies, the result of a search for love and acceptance, a search for their lost selves.

Listen to the angry, bitter words spoken by a couple who once vowed to love, honor, and respect one another. Listen as selfish demands obscure their recognition of each other's needs.

Listen to the moans of the drug addicts, the homeless, the downcast. Listen to the excuses of the overworked, the driven, the dishonest.

Listen to the groans of a lost world.

But listen also for a Voice of hope. In the middle of the chaos, His Voice can still be heard, saying, *"For the Son of Man came to seek and to save what was lost"* (Luke 19:10).

Some of us have heard this Voice. In this lost world, we have been found. We have admitted that the restlessness of our souls can be stilled only by a return to our God. We have discovered our need for God and have given up our sins for His way—a better way, based on truth, hope, and justice. Like a bride longing for the return of her betrothed, we await the coming of our Lord with a breathlessness impossible to describe. We know the Redeemer, Jesus Christ, who bore our sins on a cross and opened the way for us to be found...to be reconnected to the Father and to one another. As Isaiah 55:6 teaches, we have sought the Lord while He may be found; we have called upon Him while He is near. We have been saved.

Why then is there so little difference between the church and the unchurched, the lost and the found, the faithful and the faithless? At a time when there may be more professions of faith than ever before, why has the church lost its impact? Why are there so many decisions for Christ with so few commitments to Christ?

Why is the lostness of the world so descriptive of the church itself? Why are there as many teenage pregnancies and marital break-ups in the church as there are in the world?

Why is it that out of ten self-described Christians only one claims that his or her spiritual growth is a high priority in life?

Could it be that some of us are actually lost in church? Could it be that the evangelized need to be evangelized? Could it be that many in the church don't want the truth anymore?

As churches reach out to a lost world with the Gospel, many are growing. Facilities are expanding. Church budgets are mounting. Directional signs are being erected to guide newcomers trying to find their way.

My prayer is that this book will serve as such a sign—not for the unchurched, but for the lost in church. I want to speak specifically about some tough issues that we can't afford to ignore. The apostle Paul's admonition to believers in the early church applies to us today: *"Continue to work out your salvation with fear and trembling, for it is God who works in you to will and to act according to his good purpose"* (Phil. 2:12–13).

My concern is not only that the lost in church would be found, but also that having been truly found, we may more effectively reach our lost world with God's healing grace. Second Chronicles 7:14 promises,

> *If my people, who are called by my name, will humble themselves and pray and seek my face and turn from their wicked ways, then will I hear from heaven and will forgive their sin and will heal their land.*

This book is not for the individual who is comfortable with the status quo of Christianity. It is meant for the lost as well as the saved who are searching for the God of

the Bible and who will not rest until they have found the truth—God's truth.

My prayer is that the Son of Man will continue to seek and save the lost—whether it be the lost in the world or the lost in church.

Chapter One

The Drought

"[The Lord] leads me beside quiet waters,
he restores my soul."
—Psalm 23:2–3

A drought is sweeping our land today—from the sun-drenched coast of California to the icy shores of Massachusetts. The barrenness stretches from Antarctica to Aruba and from Zambia to Zimbabwe. No amount of rain, sleet, or snow can relieve this drought. Only the water of the Word of God can quench our thirsty spirits and bring life from death.

During nearly fifteen years of weather forecasting, I have seen hurricanes decimate towns, tornadoes obliterate homes, and blizzards close down entire states. Countless lives are destroyed by these weather beasts, yet many do not realize that lightning kills more people every year than tornadoes, hurricanes, and blizzards combined. People don't take lightning as seriously as they should. When you hear thunder, do you rush indoors and seek shelter, or do you casually wind up your activities and stroll inside unaware of the danger lurking above you? When it comes to weather, we don't always clearly see the danger on the horizon.

Nor do we take the danger of not reading the Bible seriously enough. We know that we should read the Word, yet there is always something more pressing, something that just cannot wait that we do instead. What we know in our heads seldom penetrates our hearts, leaving us in danger—a danger we all too often dismiss. A biblical drought is sweeping our world, and many in the church cannot see the danger. They ignore the consequences of neglecting God's Word.

The world is under siege by an enemy that has but one good attribute: patience. Of course, the forces of evil do not use patience to advance the kingdom of God; they use it to further the kingdom of Satan. Every day they persuade churchgoers to neglect reading the Word. As a result, people slip further and further away from their heavenly Father. He longs to speak to us through His Word, yet many say by their actions, "Sorry. Not today. I have more important things to do."

Many will read bits and pieces of the Bible without allowing it to affect their attitudes and actions. The truths of Scripture go in one ear and out the other without reaching their hearts. And even if they do understand Scripture, are they acting on it? You see, if you believe the Bible, its truths will change the way you live. Are you reading and studying the Word of God on a daily basis? If not, by your very actions you are telling God and the rest of the world, "I do not really believe the Bible." Many are lost in church because they have never drenched their minds and spirits with the water of life, the Word of God.

Droughts don't suddenly appear out of nowhere; they develop slowly. Day by day, they squeeze the life out of the land. Grass gradually loses its verdure and turns brown. You can't see it happening in an instant; shrubs and trees do not suddenly succumb to the lack of water. Weeks or months may pass before you perceive the changes. Then you say, "What happened? Everything is dead!"

That word picture aptly describes the lukewarm Christian. The lost in church are withering from a lack of spiritual water: the Bible. They are depressed, angry, and spiritually depleted. They are dry and parched in their souls, longing for something to quench their thirst. Unfortunately, few realize they are being drawn by the Holy Spirit and that they need to be washed and nourished by the everlasting spring of life-giving water. As Scripture tells us, *"Husbands, love your wives, just as Christ loved the church and gave himself up for her to make her holy, cleansing her by the washing with water through the word"* (Eph. 5:25–26); and, *"Whoever is thirsty, let him come; and whoever wishes, let him take the free gift of the water of life"* (Rev. 22:17).

Scripture clearly teaches that reading the Bible is essential for Christians. When you read the Bible, you are hearing God speak to you personally. Can you picture yourself in a desert with no water? Without water, you would die. Take that picture and apply it to the Bible. When you refuse to open the Bible, then wonder why life isn't what you expected, it's much like standing in the middle of a barren desert. A passing traveler offers you a cup of cold water, but you say, "No, thanks. I'm not thirsty." After refusing the water, you scoop up some hot sand and cradle it in both hands. You tilt the sand toward your mouth and drink it as if it were water. Choking and disillusioned, you glare at the departing traveler and sarcastically shout, "Thanks for the help!"

Water is essential to life; in fact, most humans can survive only three days without it. Without water, our bodies dehydrate. This is simple science. The sad reality for many today is that they are refusing to replenish their souls and spirits with the water of the Word; therefore, they are unable to live the abundant, fruitful life that the Lord wants them to live.

Hebrews 4:12 describes the Bible as "living and active. Sharper than any double-edged sword, it penetrates even to dividing soul and spirit, joints and marrow; it judges the thoughts and attitudes of the heart."

Where are you in your walk with the Lord? Do you understand the importance and necessity of hearing from your Father in heaven on a regular basis? Why aren't you doing it? Too busy? Are worldly desires crowding and distracting your mind?

The Lord wants to perform life-saving surgery on the lost in church, but like any reputable physician, He requires the patient's permission to begin. People need to ask for His help! Through His Word and His Holy Spirit, He wants to change the way people think and, of course, the way they act. When you study His Word and take it to heart, you are literally empowering God to act through you. God surgically removes the cancerous tumor called sin and replaces it with Himself, His Holy Spirit. You shed the old man of sin and rebellion and replace it with the fruit of the spirit.

My conversion story is somewhat different from that of the average Christian. While most people get saved sitting in church, or being led to the Lord by another Christian, I was born again by reading the Word of God. No preacher fed me the truth; no one explained the plan of salvation. Instead, it was the Lord and I, one-on-one. His voice softly filled my heart as I read and studied the Bible. The Word of God exposed my sin and showed me how God wanted to change me from the inside out.

Through His Word, I learned the most important information available to mankind. It was as if Jesus Christ, the Creator of the universe, sat beside me and told me about Himself. He told me about His life on earth, the miracles, the temptations, and the cruel cross. He explained how He created the world and why He wanted a personal relationship with me. Jesus taught me history, or better yet, "His Story."

He has not only given me a window into the past, but He has also shown me the future. As the world spirals toward the end times, are you prepared to meet your Maker? The lost in church are woefully unprepared for the future. They do not read the Bible on a consistent basis, which leaves them open prey to a strong, powerful enemy.

Why do some people catch on fire for the Lord and others don't? The simple explanation lies with the Word. A person spending time with Jesus, reading and ingesting the Word of hope, benefits from that time with the Master.

We are like an appliance needing electricity to operate. Unless we plug into the outlet, Jesus Christ, we cannot function properly. He is our energy, our power, our force, our hope in living. Without Him, we are useless, unable to function as designed by our Creator.

Psalm 119:9 reminds us, *"How can a young man keep his way pure? By living according to your word."* This concept isn't something new or revolutionary. Thousands and thousands of years ago, writers of the Old Testament wrote of this spiritual truth. Moses penned these words from Deuteronomy 32:46–47:

> *Set your hearts on all the words which I testify among you today, which you shall command your children to be careful to observe; all the words of this law. For it is not a futile thing for you, because it is your life.* (NKJV)

Wow! If that thought doesn't get you excited, then you might want to check your pulse. The words Moses spoke were straight from the throne of God Almighty. Can you imagine it? In the middle of the desert, before reaching the Promised Land, the entire nation of Israel was standing before Moses, needing direction and hope, wanting to hear from God.

First, Moses told them to *"set [their] hearts."* Picture some workers outside your home laying down a new concrete driveway. You watch as the gray liquid flows easily from the truck and splashes on the ground. Several men push the concrete into place and mold it with their tools. The following day you stroll out your front door and walk toward your new driveway. You stop at the edge and wonder if it's dry. Gently, you reach down and touch the new surface. It feels hard, so you place your full weight on it and walk around. Obviously, the concrete is "set" in place.

Do you see the picture? The molding of that concrete is like Jesus and His Word. He shapes you into His image, forming a new creation. Once the Word fills and molds you, your heart will be "set" on Him. Your faith will not be moved or shaken by life's certain troubles. Just as that concrete is hard and strong, your faith will be solid. Simply put, stick to Jesus like that concrete sticks to itself. Without the Bible, your spiritual concrete will never set. You'll never be capable of living the Christian life or obeying Jesus.

Then Moses told the Israelites to *"be careful to observe."* How can people carefully observe the words of the Lord if they don't know them? A person carefully observing the Word of God will hold it in high regard and take it seriously. Jesus does the majority of His life-changing work through the awesome power of His Word. We are to observe, or obey, His commands. We can't do this unless we read God's Word.

What were the Israelites to observe and set their hearts on? *"All the words of this law."* The word *"all"* was used intentionally. The lost in church love to choose which commands they will obey. If some part isn't convenient, or if it requires too much work on their parts, many simply discard or ignore those truths. They may say, "I'll have to pray about that"; yet, inwardly, they have already made up their minds to disobey, figuring God is a loving, forgiving God. You can trust all of God's Word just as you can trust God with every part of your life.

The next part of the verse says, *"It is not a futile thing."* The *New International Version* uses the word *"idle."* I don't know many Christians who would openly say the Bible is full of idle, futile, meaningless words. However, let's examine not words or thoughts, but actions. Our belief system is revealed by what we do. In other words, deeds are based on faith. What is in a heart comes out in a person's life. As Luke 6:43–45 says,

> *No good tree bears bad fruit, nor does a bad tree bear good fruit. Each tree is recognized by its own fruit. People do not pick figs from thornbushes, or grapes from briers. The good man brings good things out of the good stored up in his heart, and the evil man brings evil things out of the evil stored up in his heart. For out of the overflow of his heart his mouth speaks.*

If the church is not consistently in the Word of God, it will be only a shell without foundation or substance. Knowing God is knowing His Word. Having faith is obeying God.

"It is your life." Can the Lord be any clearer? Apart from Jesus and His Word, eternal life cannot be achieved, for we all sin and *"fall short of the glory of God"* (Rom. 3:23). When you look at your Bible, what do you think? Do you treat it like the very words of God? Don't try to substitute your pastor, your church, your Christian friends, your spouse, or anything else in this world for the Word of God! First Samuel 3:7 says, *"Now Samuel did not yet know the LORD: The word of the LORD had not yet been revealed to him."* Verse 21 adds, *"The LORD continued to appear at Shiloh, and there he revealed himself to Samuel through his word."* God longs to give the lost in church life—real life—eternal life. It comes only through Jesus Christ who reveals Himself through the Holy Spirit and Scripture.

God wants to shatter the comfort zones of those lost in church, the mind-set that says, "I hear from God when the preacher is talking. What more do you expect of me?" God expects a lot more of you than an hour or two a week. Try giving your spouse that much time and see where it gets you. You cannot bear fruit for God apart from the indwelling of the Holy Spirit through the transforming of your mind and heart, and that transformation comes through studying the Bible and obeying the voice of the Spirit.

Before Saul became king of Israel, he had an interesting conversation with the prophet Samuel, who told him, *"The Spirit of the LORD will come upon you in power, and you will prophesy with them; and you will be changed into a different person"* (1 Sam. 10:6). When the Word of the all-powerful King of the universe indwells you, you will be a different man or woman, shedding the sinful past of yesterday to fulfill a spiritually rich future.

How can you become more righteous and fruitful in your life? Psalm 119:11 shows the way: *"I have hidden your word in my heart that I might not sin against you."* The Bible has the power to create a completely new individual: a person who is happy, content, and full of wisdom. Picture the Bible as a computer disk. You are the computer, and God is the Programmer. He longs to remove the old disk, which is corrupted and useless, and replace it with a perfect disk, His Holy Word.

Jesus Christ is searching for men and women who really want to hear His voice. Too many in the church like to think that they hear God's voice in the circumstances of their lives, yet, in truth, they are hearing the static of the devil. Let me explain. How many times have you heard someone say, "God wants this to happen," or "God told me I would get that job," or "It's God's will that my life will improve." We love to believe that we have this special connection to God, and we make sure everybody around us knows it. We want to believe that God will never allow any bad things to happen to us and that Christianity is the golden road to Oz.

Countless people today fall into this religious trap, unwilling and unable to come to a knowledge of the truth. How does one know what God really wants when he doesn't cuddle up beside Him and listen to His voice? How can a person claim a special relationship with Christ when he refuses to communicate in any meaningful manner with Him? Why do people think God is going to bless them when they shun His Word and His commandments? If you want to have a special relationship with God, pick up His heavenly phone—the Bible—and listen to what He wants to say to you. Before King David died, he exhorted his son with these words:

> And you, my son Solomon, acknowledge the God of your father, and serve him with wholehearted devotion and with a willing mind, for the LORD searches every heart and understands every motive behind the thoughts. If you seek him, he will be found by you; but if you forsake him, he will reject you forever.
>
> (1 Chron. 28:9)

God longs for a special relationship with you; His greatest desire is to fellowship with you. Some like to think that God doesn't see what they do or hear what they say. They don't delve into the Bible because they are hiding from God, fearful of what they might learn. To those who are unsaved or backslidden, it certainly is scary to realize that God is watching your every move, your every thought, your every attitude. For many lost in church today, the most comfortable thing to do is hide, to pretend He's not watching. They resort to our first parents' behavior. After disobeying God, Adam and Eve did what came naturally to sinners. Genesis 3:8–14 tells the story:

> Then the man and his wife heard the sound of the LORD God as he was walking in the garden in the cool of the day, and they hid from the LORD God among the trees of the garden. But the LORD God called to the man, "Where are you?" He answered, "I heard you in the garden, and I was afraid because I was naked; so I

hid." And he said, "Who told you that you were naked? Have you eaten from the tree that I commanded you not to eat from?" The man said, "The woman you put here with me—she gave me some fruit from the tree, and I ate it." Then the LORD God said to the woman, "What is this you have done?" The woman said, "The serpent deceived me, and I ate." So the LORD God said to the serpent, "Because you have done this, cursed are you above all the livestock and all the wild animals! You will crawl on your belly and you will eat dust all the days of your life." (Gen. 3:8–14)

Did you catch it? Adam and Eve's first reaction was to hide from God. God's response was to find them and confront them. If you are ignoring the Word of God by not reading and studying it, or not obeying it, God will continue to seek you. You can run, but you cannot hide from God. The lost in church are hiding behind their church membership, their good deeds, their parents' walk with God, or other flimsy excuses that will not be accepted by a holy God.

Kids are a perfect example of this tendency to hide. When being disciplined, my oldest child, Christina, loved to go into her favorite corner, crouch behind a big rocking chair, and bury her head. She simply wanted to be left alone. She didn't want any kind of spotlight on her; she preferred the solitude. Christina wanted to hide in hopes the storm would pass, that it would all go away.

Everybody has his favorite hiding place. The lost in church try to hide from God by steering clear of His Word; they also tend to blame others as Adam and Eve did. Adam tried to excuse his sin by putting the blame onto Eve. He even had the audacity to accuse God Himself when he said, *"The woman you put here with me— she gave me some fruit from the tree, and I ate it"* (Gen. 3:12). Eve didn't want to accept personal responsibility for her actions either; she blamed the serpent. Are you blaming somebody or something for your neglect of God's

Word: your spouse, your children, your work schedule, your involvement in church activities? Are you a driven businessman who puts your work before God? Are you a stressed-out wife who gives her all to the care of her children and home? What's your first priority? Please understand that God expects to be your first priority, period! The simplest definition of idolatry is putting anything or anyone above God in any way, shape, or form.

There's an astonishingly bizarre attitude among many churchgoers today. What they say they know, they don't do. They understand the importance of spending time in their Bibles, yet their consciences don't seem to stop them from ignoring this truth. First Timothy 4:1–2 speaks to this attitude:

> *The Spirit clearly says that in later times some will abandon the faith and follow deceiving spirits and things taught by demons. Such teachings come through hypocritical liars, whose consciences have been seared as with a hot iron.*

In other words, many lost in church can be compared to religious hypocrites who unknowingly listen to the devil instead of God. They can't represent God because they don't have a personal relationship with Him. They are unwilling to listen to Him. They have said no to the Holy Spirit so many times that their consciences cannot detect God's rebukes. To put it bluntly, they can't tell the difference between the voice of God and the voice of Satan. Think of it this way. The radio frequency of God flows through His Word and His Holy Spirit. Other stations broadcast spiritual propaganda and try to mimic God's message. Yet there is only one Voice and one Book that can fill your soul with the truth that can change your life forever.

A spiritual war of biblical magnitude is assaulting the world today, and many in the church are saying, "What war?" They have no armor or weapons to fight effectively.

Instead, they fight among themselves rather than against the forces of evil. This is a tragedy.

What do you think when you hear the word *relationship?* Most think of an intimate friendship or a deep companionship. But what does it take for a relationship to work? How do we achieve a vital bond with our God, our families, our friends? In order for a relationship to grow and thrive, there must be good communication. The lost in church do not have their communication lines open to God; instead, the dial tones of their spiritual receivers are dead, or faint, at best.

Several years ago, I was tracking a powerful hurricane through the Caribbean all morning long. My bosses had been hovering like hawks over the weather center, wanting to know if we were going to get hit. After a grueling day, I was finally able to go home. As I entered our foyer, I caught a glimpse of my wife sitting on the couch in the living room.

"Hey, honey," I mumbled, rubbing my aching back.

Her voice sounded downcast as she called out, "Jon, can you come in here and talk to me?"

I took a deep breath as I headed for the stairs.

"Sure. Just let me get out of these dress clothes."

I dragged myself up the stairs without another word from my wife, Tina. Several minutes later, I entered the living room, wearing my jeans and favorite battered sweatshirt. I sat down on the chair opposite her and reached for the remote control.

"What are you doing?" she asked.

Without looking at her, I responded, "Just want to get a quick update on the hurricane. Won't take too long."

With the hurricane days if not a week away, I didn't need to do this at that moment.

"This is important!" Tina said, her voice trembling.

"I know, I know. I promise it won't take long."

I focused on the spinning cyclone as the meteorologist reported the up-to-date information. I didn't notice the sad yet stormy glare staring back at me. When the report ended, I flipped off the television and leaned back against the soft cushion.

"So what's up?" My nonchalant attitude wasn't scoring any points.

Tina struggled to be patient as she tried to overlook my insensitivity.

"I wanted to talk to you about something that's really important to me. You see..."

My ears tuned her out as I recalled a tennis match that was being broadcast live on television. I reached for the remote control.

"What are you doing?" She was mad as a hornet.

As I punched the channels on the remote, I glanced her way. "I'm sorry, honey bunny. I just want to see what's happening in the tennis match I told you about."

My wife stood up with fists clenched. She mumbled something I didn't hear as she left the room.

Obviously, the storm inside my home was of my own making. Yes, I was insensitive, unloving, uncaring, and unsympathetic. In other words, I was a jerk. Are you ready for a revelation? I didn't want to hear her voice. I didn't want to communicate with her right then. Oh, yes, I could pretend that wasn't true, but by my actions, I said, "You are not important to me right now. Go away!"

Christians are in a relationship with God, and communication is essential for that relationship to grow. When we pray, we are talking to God, telling Him our deepest desires and yearnings, laying our hearts and souls before His throne. When we read the Bible, God talks to us, one-on-one, in an intimate way. But when we refuse to read and study His Word, we are acting as I did with my wife. She was rightfully angry that I wouldn't give her my undivided attention. My selfish devotion to my job and hobbies robbed my wife of what she needed most...me.

Do you see it now? God wants to speak to you more than you can possibly imagine. The lost in church need to stop looking toward heaven and saying, "Not today, God. Sorry. No time! Things to do, people to see, places to go. Maybe tomorrow." The drought of the Word of God is a self-imposed plague that can be healed if the church will take the time to hear from God.

The Word of God is food for the soul. John 4:32–34 says,

> Meanwhile his disciples urged him, "Rabbi, eat something." But he said to them, "I have food to eat that you know nothing about." Then his disciples said to each other, "Could someone have brought him food?" "My food," said Jesus, "is to do the will of him who sent me and to finish his work."

Even the disciples had trouble understanding the connection between food for the body and food for the soul. John 6:48–51 says,

> I am the bread of life. Your forefathers ate the manna in the desert, yet they died. But here is the bread that comes down from heaven, which a man may eat and not die. I am the living bread that came down from heaven. If anyone eats of this bread, he will live forever. This bread is my flesh, which I will give for the life of the world.

Combine these verses with John 1:1, "In the beginning was the Word, and the Word was with God, and the Word was God," and verse 14, "The Word became flesh and made his dwelling among us," and you see a picture of Jesus Christ of Nazareth as the spiritual food of the Christian. Simply put, the words in the Bible are the words of Jesus. With them, you live; without them, you die.

What does God see when He looks at the modern church? Does He see humble saints hungry for His voice? I believe that too often God sees people starving and malnourished, hobbling along in life with little or no direction, weakened by a lack of spiritual food.

Each Sunday, many come to church without having eaten any spiritual food all week. Before the altar, a giant buffet is spread before them. The mere smell of the food makes them salivate. Many are feeling delirious as their stomachs cry out from hunger. Suddenly, the pastor motions for the people to come forward. The famished rush toward the food. The pastor sees the flock crashing toward him like a tidal wave, and he lunges out of the way in the nick of time. There's complete chaos as the hungry masses gorge themselves. Food flies everywhere; it's every person for himself.

What's happening here? It's a look at the church today. Can you imagine lasting a week without food? Many in the church haven't read their Bibles all week; they are spiritually empty. Too many go to church on Sunday morning, open their Bibles, and then close them until the following week. Maybe they read a few verses now and then to relieve their burnt consciences, but this spiritual "snack" won't satisfy their empty hearts and souls. God longs for deep, honest conversations with His loved ones, but too often, He gets only passing glances or self-righteous nods. Of course, this type of sparse communication could never support a healthy marriage on earth, let alone sustain a relationship with the Maker of heaven.

Hebrews 5:12–14 convicts many when it says,

Though by this time you ought to be teachers, you need someone to teach you the elementary truths of God's word all over again. You need milk, not solid food! Anyone who lives on milk, being still an infant, is not acquainted with the teaching about righteousness. But solid food is for the mature, who by constant use have trained themselves to distinguish good from evil.

Ouch! Where are you in your spiritual walk? Too many Christians today are mere babes in Christ when they should be adults who are caring for others. I have two children, and I remember how cute and cuddly they were as babies. They are certainly gifts from God, but they had to be taken care of twenty-four hours a day, seven days a week. God doesn't want the church to be composed of just babies, always taking and never giving. Spiritual infants who should have grown up long ago drain the church. Instead, He wants Christians to use their gifts to build strong families, to serve their communities, and to strengthen the kingdom of God. Without the Word of God richly indwelling the church through the Holy Spirit, those in church will fail their cities, their churches, their families, and their God.

The Old Testament records how Israel consistently turned its back on God. It happened again during Elijah's day. The Israelites were backslidden, corrupt, and because of their evil ways, God had smitten them with a terrible drought. Then the prophet summoned King Ahab and the people of Israel to gather for a challenge. First Kings 18:21 says, *"Elijah went before the people and said, 'How long will you waver between two opinions? If the LORD is God, follow him; but if Baal is God, follow him.' But the people said nothing."*

Like these Israelites of old, many in the church are torn between two opinions. Too many are living like the world, ignoring their Bibles and their Savior. Lost in church, they go to services expecting nothing more than the traditional songs and an encouraging sermon from the pastor. They are caught between the sinful highs of this world and the message of the cross. They try to live with one foot in the world and the other in the church. God abhors this type of double-mindedness. He hated it four thousand years ago, and He hates it today.

The Old Testament story says that the people didn't respond to Elijah. In essence, they were speechless. They knew they were wrong, so what could they say? No matter what your spiritual status is, God wants those divided in heart and mind to repent and change their ways. God's forgiveness comes to us when we have a repentant heart. Remember, teetering on the faith fence is dangerous! Reading and studying the Bible is critical to your spiritual journey.

The most difficult crowd to reach with the true gospel of Jesus Christ is the religious crowd. The lost in church assume they are going to heaven, almost taking it for granted as their birthright. Appearing to be religious is not good enough. As Jesus said to the so-called religious of His day,

> *"If you hold to my teaching, you are really my disciples. Then you will know the truth, and the truth will set you free." They answered him, "We are Abraham's descendants and have never been slaves of anyone. How can you say that we shall be set free?"* (John 8:31–33)

He answered, *"I know you are Abraham's descendants. Yet you are ready to kill me, because you have no room for my word"* (v. 37).

What place does the Bible hold in your life? People who love Jesus, who are saved from an eternity in hell, love His Word. They want to know what God has to say to them. Reading and studying His Word is a priority in their lives.

Are you thirsty for righteousness? There's only one place to go to be satisfied. God's Word is waiting for you. Open it, drink in His truths, and be saturated with His presence. The remedy for a spiritual drought is waiting for you in the pages of God's Word.

Chapter Two

Needed: Repentance in the Pews

"I know your deeds, that you are neither cold nor hot.
I wish you were either one or the other! So, because you
are lukewarm—neither hot nor cold—I am about
to spit you out of my mouth."
—Revelation 3:15–16

The word *lukewarm* occurs only once in Scripture, yet its meaning and implications are recorded in nearly every one of the books of the Bible. What does it mean to be lukewarm? What can we do if we fall into this compromised mind-set?

In this passage from Revelation, Jesus was speaking to the church in Laodicea. He said, *"'I know your deeds.'* I can see right through you! I know what you have done, what you are doing, and what you are going to do. I know what you are thinking and how you are feeling. You may be able to fool others and even fool yourself, but you can't fool Me."

God sees all, hears all, and knows all. When He examines the church, He sees three types of people: the hot, the cold, and the lukewarm.

People who are *hot* are on fire for the Lord. The Holy Spirit has dominion in their lives. They may have experienced fiery trials, but they have come through with a stronger faith and a more committed determination to serve the Lord. They are not perfect, but they are striving for the perfection that only the Lord can give. They take the words of Jesus seriously: *"Be perfect, therefore, as your heavenly Father is perfect"* (Matt. 5:48). Jesus Christ rules in their lives, and His light shines through them.

Those who are *cold* have knowingly or unknowingly rejected God. Since Jesus was talking to the *church* of Laodicea, we can assume that this type of people can be found in the pews. They are not saved nor do they want to be. They are more concerned with man's opinion than with God's. It's doubtful that they are vocal about their faith since they have so little. They don't talk to others about Jesus, and they don't allow His words to affect their actions. They go to church to be seen by others, possibly to advance their own agendas or to quiet their nagging consciences.

The third category is the *lukewarm.* They are best described as outwardly religious, yet uncommitted and self-complacent. They are indifferent toward the Lord, not *"fervent in spirit"* (Rom. 12:11 NKJV). Equally bad is the fact that they are ignorant of their pathetic condition. They rely on church membership to prove their religiosity, but they refuse to give their lives wholeheartedly to the Savior. They are part-time in their faith, casual in their walk, and unsettled in their hearts. Deep down they know something isn't right, but they take comfort in their rituals. Many will die and go into eternity without Christ. When asked why they should be admitted to heaven, here are some of the answers they will offer at the Great White Throne:

- I was a good person.
- I was a faithful Baptist (or Catholic, Methodist, Lutheran, Charismatic, Episcopalian...).
- I was a member of my church since I was a kid.
- I was baptized.
- I was a deacon.
- I walked the aisle when I was a teenager.
- I really tried to do the right thing.
- I taught kids in Sunday school.

None of these answers will satisfy the Lord on Judgment Day. Scripture is clear: You must be one of His sheep. You must know His voice and respond to it in obedience.

Jesus' judgment against the church of Laodicea was that they were lukewarm. The church had taken on the characteristics of its city. Rather than being *"transformed"* (Rom. 12:2), they had *conformed* to the world around them. They were content with what they had; they thought they lacked nothing.

Laodicea was located in the middle of the vast Roman Empire. It was a wealthy city with strong financial assets that came from trade and the production of black glossy wool. It also was noted for its school of medicine, which produced a healing ointment for the eyes known as Phrygian powder. But for all its prosperity, this city had one major problem: poor drinking water. Nearly all the small rivers and streams came from hot springs. These hot springs were filled with impurities that could cause various types of sickness. This picture of dirty, warm, unpalatable water has a spiritual application. Just as this kind of water offers little relief to physical thirst, so a lukewarm faith offers a poor remedy for spiritual thirst.

What follows in this passage from Revelation is one of the most profound, controversial verses in all the Word of God. Jesus says, *"I could wish you were cold or hot"* (Rev. 3:15 NKJV). The *New International Version* says, *"I wish you were either one or the other!"*

God is making a dramatic statement about the lukewarm church today. Simply put, He's saying lukewarm Christianity is not an option. We know Scripture emphatically declares that God doesn't want anybody to lose his soul; therefore, we must conclude that God wants everybody to be "on fire" for Him. What happens when somebody refuses to be "hot"? Gradually, he will become lukewarm. If you reject true Christianity, if you refuse to take up your cross or to surrender your life, then God would rather you fall over to the "cold" side! Do you find that statement controversial? Does it bother you to hear it stated that way?

People who give God the cold shoulder do not harm the kingdom of God as much as those who are lukewarm. Those who are cold are non-players; they are non-combatants in a spiritual war that will soon end with the second coming of Christ. These people are on the sidelines, oblivious to the meaning of life and death. A person who is cold cannot spread hypocrisy like one who is lukewarm.

Hypocrisy does incredible damage to Christianity and the name of Christ. Although liberal groups, other religions, atheists, and agnostics have played a part in the thwarting of Christianity, I believe the greatest damage is inflicted from the pews in the lukewarm church. A complacent attitude toward Christ will result in devastating consequences.

Continuing from the third chapter of Revelation we see God's verdict on the lukewarm church. He says, *"I am about to spit you out of my mouth"* (v. 16).

Literally speaking, the word *"spit"* (*"spue"* KJV) means to vomit. What's God saying? How can we understand this rebuke for today's church and apply it to our lives? Let's start with a lesson from biology. A person who is vomiting is getting rid of some type of poison in his system. Though vomiting is anything but pleasant, it's an effective defense mechanism your body employs. It rids the body of harmful bacteria and chemicals that can harm or even kill a person.

Lukewarm Christianity is poison to the body of Christ. It's an invader from the enemy, and it's harmful. Jesus doesn't mince words. He wants our attention. If every lukewarm Christian were to renounce his sin, repent, and eagerly seek the face of God, this world would be a vastly better place. Instead of God's curses upon our land, His blessings would overflow in our lives.

Revelation 3:17 describes the lukewarm person: *"You say, 'I am rich; I have acquired wealth and do not need a thing.'"* Can these words be attributed to a Christian? Notice this person's attitude, his way of thinking. He is materialistic, which is an indictment of so many in the pews today. Many are more interested in their 401(k) plans for retirement on earth than in their eternal retirement in heaven. Do you think more about money than God? Do you put more energy and time into your last earthly years than into your everlasting spiritual years? It's sad but often true: When we have everything we need and most of what we want, it's then that we forget God. Have we forsaken Jesus Christ for the almighty dollar? We'll examine this problem further in Chapter Four.

Although these people described themselves as needing nothing, Jesus saw their true condition. They were lacking the basics. He called them *"wretched, pitiful, poor, blind and naked"* (Rev. 3:17). Let's look at each of these characteristics.

"Wretched." Paul used this same word in Romans 7:24 to describe the flesh-ruled self: *"What a wretched man I am! Who will rescue me from this body of death?"* Sadly, the Laodiceans were unaware of their sinful condition; their ignorance led to spiritual apathy. Rather than being Christ-reliant, they were self-reliant. Holiness was foreign to them. They did not take seriously the admonition in Hebrews 12:14 to *"pursue peace with all people, and holiness, without which no one will see the Lord"* (NKJV).

"Pitiful." The Laodiceans were proud of their accomplishments. They boasted that they had *"acquired wealth."* Yet Jesus recognized them for what they were. *"Pitiful"* (*"miserable"* NKJV) people are lonely, sad, and often depressed. God's joy and peace cannot reside in them because of their persistent, unrepentant sin. They have heard of the *"joy of the LORD"* (Neh. 8:10), but they cannot

grasp its meaning with their darkened hearts. Jesus, the Author of Life, has no place in their lives because they stubbornly reject the cost of being Christ's disciple.

Remember the rich young man who came to Jesus? He asked, *"What good thing must I do to get eternal life?"* (Matt. 19:16). If you were to believe his testimony, in many ways he was perfect. But one area of his life kept him from the grace of God. When he approached Jesus, he wanted to know what he must do to inherit eternal life. He didn't expect Jesus' response. Jesus told him, *"If you want to be perfect, go, sell your possessions and give to the poor, and you will have treasure in heaven. Then come, follow me"* (Matt. 19:21). The following verse reveals this man's heart. *"When the young man heard this, he went away sad, because he had great wealth."* That rich young man was miserable because he knew he didn't have what it takes to follow Christ, and he refused to allow God to change his sad condition! Do we really understand what God requires? He expects us to "count the cost" before we call on His name. As Christians, we cannot hold anything back from the Lord. Loving and obeying Him must be our first priority.

"Poor." Lukewarm Christians see their great worldly wealth and think they have it made. Nothing can hurt them. At the beginning of Jesus' ministry, He came to a synagogue in His hometown of Nazareth. He opened a scroll from the book of Isaiah and began to read a prophecy about Himself to the crowd.

> The Spirit of the Lord GOD is upon Me, because the LORD has anointed Me to preach good tidings to the poor; He has sent Me to heal the brokenhearted, to proclaim liberty to the captives, and the opening of the prison to those who are bound; to proclaim the acceptable year of the LORD. (Isa. 61:1–2 NKJV)

Please do not envision a destitute person living in earthly poverty. God's definition of *poor* has nothing to do with what's in your bank account, but rather what's in your heart. Poor people are brokenhearted. They need deliverance. They are oppressed and need God's salvation. They don't have God in their lives to enrich them spiritually, to guide them in the ways of righteousness, and to touch them in ways that only He can. Poor people don't possess the riches of God's grace.

"Blind." Imagine you've lost your eyesight. Without the aid of your family or friends, without a cane or a Seeing Eye dog, you attempt to leave your house. You do a good job of getting to your front door. Slowly, carefully, you maneuver down your steps. Once you reach the busy street in front of your house, you hear something that stops you dead in your tracks. It's rush hour Monday morning; cars are speeding by you. After standing there for several minutes, you sense a lull in the traffic. Taking a deep gulp, you begin to sprint across the pavement. Suddenly you hear the sounds of squealing tires and honking horns. You panic and stop in the middle of the road; you're frozen in fear. You wonder if you're going to die. Frantic, you realize nobody is there to help you. No one is there to guide you to safety.

What a sad story! God paints a picture with the word *"blind."* The spiritually blind can't see the road ahead. They can't see God trying to get their attention to guide them safely though life's dangerous roadways. They can't hear God's voice directing them to stop or to proceed. They stumble through life unable to discern good from evil, right from wrong, and God from gods. They feel alone because they have blockaded the Lord from their lives. Do you remember Paul's conversion on the road to Damascus? God had to blind him to get his attention, but once He did, Paul surrendered to Christ, and, as a result, turned the Roman Empire upside down. A new Christian convert is often as excited as a blind person who has just regained his eyesight. There's nothing more exciting than seeing and living the truth.

"*Naked.*" Did you know that Christians will receive a white robe in heaven? You don't have any righteousness of your own to dress in. Scripture says, "*All our righteous acts are like filthy rags*" (Isa. 64:6), yet we can be dressed in the "*righteousness that comes from God and is by faith*" (Phil. 3:9). Revelation 7:9 gives us a glimpse of this blessed event.

> *After these things I looked, and behold, a great multitude which no one could number, of all nations, tribes, peoples, and tongues, standing before the throne and before the Lamb, clothed with white robes, with palm branches in their hands.* (NKJV)

Only the blood of Jesus can atone for and cover our sins. When we stand before the Judgment Seat of Christ, God will allow only those wearing white robes to enter heaven. If you are dressed in His righteousness—in your white robe—then you're forgiven, and paradise is yours.

Adam and Eve had perfect fellowship with God. They were sinless before God with all eternity before them. What a wonderful picture...until they fell for the great lie of Satan. Genesis 3:6–7 says,

> *When the woman saw that the fruit of the tree was good for food and pleasing to the eye, and also desirable for gaining wisdom, she took some and ate it. She also gave some to her husband, who was with her, and he ate it. Then the eyes of both of them were opened, and they realized they were naked; so they sewed fig leaves together and made coverings for themselves.*

When the first couple sinned, they were suddenly aware of their nakedness. They were exposed before God, guilty of transgression and destined for a life far different from the one to which they had grown accustomed. Do you feel naked or ashamed before God? Do you want to run away from Him like a person who suddenly finds himself naked in front of a crowd? God wants us to worship Him in truth and spirit, not in shame and cowardice.

Revelation 3:18 offers God's solution to the problem:

I counsel you to buy from me gold refined in the fire, so you can become rich; and white clothes to wear, so you can cover your shameful nakedness; and salve to put on your eyes, so you can see.

Jesus has the answer for the lukewarm church, but it isn't necessarily what they want to hear. Those who see themselves as rich yet live in spiritual poverty possess only fool's gold. You can receive God's gold, however, if you are willing to ask, seek, and knock. God wants us to search for Him; He wants to see our level of devotion and our willingness to suffer for His sake. Refined gold must be placed in the fire. The purpose is to get rid of all impurities and pollutants. Once it goes through the fire of a refinery, it's pure, spotless, and more valuable. All the other metals and minerals that were attached to it are burned off, leaving nothing but precious metal. In the same way, God doesn't allow counterfeits into heaven. Allow Him to remove your impurities and cover your nakedness. That white robe will be the most important garment you'll ever wear!

God wants to do the same thing to the lukewarm church. The Bible clearly teaches that the difficulties, trials, and persecutions we face are used by God to make us pure, spotless, and more valuable to the kingdom. Romans 5:3–4 brings this principle to light: *"We also rejoice in our sufferings, because we know that suffering produces perseverance; perseverance, character; and character, hope."*

Do you see how God works? He wants to bless you more than you can imagine, yet His blessings may not be what you expect. They may occur in ways that you weren't prepared for. God will allow trials and tribulations in your life to strengthen your faith. And that faith is spiritual gold, more valuable than anything this earth could offer. Faith often comes through tough times. Although the experiences may be painful for the moment, in the end, you will emerge stronger, wiser, and more full of faith. Simply put, God's fire often takes us through the school of hard knocks. With the right attitude and faith, you will feel richer than any millionaire, and you will be rewarded richly with all of heaven's glory.

Jesus also wants to dress us in white garments to cover our shameful nakedness. Only God can provide this clothing.

> *Finally, be strong in the Lord and in his mighty power. Put on the full armor of God so that you can take your stand against the devil's schemes. For our struggle is not against flesh and blood, but against the rulers, against the authorities, against the powers of this dark world and against the spiritual forces of evil in the heavenly realms. Therefore put on the full armor of God, so that when the day of evil comes, you may be able to stand your ground, and after you have done everything, to stand. Stand firm then, with the belt of truth buckled around your waist, with the breastplate of righteousness in place, and with your feet fitted with the readiness that comes from the gospel of peace. In addition to all this, take up the shield of faith, with which you can extinguish all the flaming arrows of the evil one. Take the helmet of salvation and the sword of the Spirit, which is the word of God.* (Eph. 6:10–17)

These verses show a fully clothed Christian who is completely prepared to withstand the devil's attacks. He has a white robe, a belt, a breastplate, shoes, a shield, and a helmet. Sadly, God looks down from heaven and sees many "religious" people in the church who are naked...totally exposed to the elements and Satan's darts.

Imagine a howling snowstorm with windchills near zero. A grandma is readying her grandchild for a fun day in the snow.

"Honey, you need to put on your warm coat," says the wise elderly lady.

The little four-year-old puckers her lips in distaste. "I don't want to wear it," she cries as she stomps her feet in protest. "I don't like the way it feels."

Her grandma is undeterred. "Don't be silly, darling. You have to put it on, or you'll get sick."

The youngster's eyes turn toward the window, mesmerized by the falling snow.

"No, I won't! I want to go outside now!"

The little girl's lack of sensibility is comical. Ignoring the child's protests, the grandma grabs the warm jacket and hands it to the girl.

"Put this on," she says gently. "And you'll need your hat, gloves, and this scarf, too."

The child throws the jacket to the floor and runs out of the house. She is not going to be told what to do; she knows it all! Her grandma runs after her calling, "Come back, honey! You're going to get sick! Please, come back!"

Can you see the naked, lukewarm church in this story? Those straddling the faith fence know so little. They're like the four-year-old—they think they know it all. But like the wise grandma, the Lord pursues us, undeterred by our foolishness. His mission is to clothe us with His righteousness. Yet in our self-conceit, we rush into the spiritual storms of life, completely unprepared for the dangers that are lurking in the world. In our nakedness, we get sick and polluted by the cold world. Like that foolish child, we shun God's own remedy, the spiritual clothing of holiness and repentance.

Still, our heavenly Father loves us. He does not abandon us in our rebellion. His discipline is a sign of His ongoing love. Revelation 43:19 states, *"As many as I love, I rebuke and chasten. Therefore be zealous and repent"*

(NKJV). One of the best ways to know if Christ is your Savior is spelled out in this verse. He disciplines His children. When His sheep stray onto one of life's many dangerous highways, Jesus will pull them off that road and chide them. All true believers are occasionally rebuked by their Lord.

The Bible specifically addresses this point in Hebrews 12:5–11:

> *"My son, do not make light of the Lord's discipline, and do not lose heart when he rebukes you, because the Lord disciplines those he loves, and he punishes everyone he accepts as a son."* *Endure hardship as discipline; God is treating you as sons. For what son is not disciplined by his father? If you are not disciplined (and everyone undergoes discipline), then you are illegitimate children and not true sons. Moreover, we have all had human fathers who disciplined us and we respected them for it. How much more should we submit to the Father of our spirits and live! Our fathers disciplined us for a little while as they thought best; but God disciplines us for our good, that we may share in his holiness. No discipline seems pleasant at the time, but painful. Later on, however, it produces a harvest of righteousness and peace for those who have been trained by it.*

When times get tough, how do we react? Do we remember that God wants to shape us and mold us into His image? When we go through life's trials, do we remember that *"in all things God works for the good of those who love him, who have been called according to his purpose"* (Rom. 8:28)? Or do we push aside the higher purposes of our lives? Instead of getting upset when trouble comes knocking, we should drop to our knees and praise the Lord through life's storms. Instead of complaining when things don't go our way, we should give each situation to God. He can turn our problems into blessings.

You may say, "Hey, everything's going great in my life! No trials, no persecution, no problems." This may be a dangerous attitude because Jesus warned us that *"in this world you will have trouble"* (John 16:33). If you don't believe that Christians must suffer for the Lord, then open your Bible! Those who don't accept the discipline of the Lord are *"illegitimate children and not true sons"* (Heb. 12:8).

The Bible explains that God's rod of discipline is for our good, not our harm. He wants to gently, and sometimes not so gently, guide us back to the right path. His discipline is in our best interest; the end result of this chastening is holiness, and holiness brings glory to God through our obedience. Think for a moment about somebody who has a terrible reputation. Would you trust him? Would you confide in him or ask for his advice? Would you want to spend time with him? Maybe you would be worried about your own reputation. Now think about God for a moment. Do you think He's concerned with His reputation? The answer is, absolutely! If the church of Jesus Christ isn't a good witness to the world, then God's reputation is impugned. As Christians, we should live in a way that reflects God's holiness and goodness to the world. We should take seriously the responsibility of bearing His name.

Consider this. If God's reputation is hurt by the church's conduct, will people—

- Trust God with their lives?
- Confide in the Lord with their deep secret sins?
- Ask God for advice?
- Want to spend time with Him?

Jesus Christ's good name can be damaged by church people who refuse to repent of their sins. Lukewarm Christianity is one of the most grievous lifestyles in the world today because it makes God look bad. Millions of people have refused God's message of love and holiness because of the actions of those who claim to follow Him. People are longing for God deep in their souls. Sometimes all they need to see is one committed, totally dedicated Christian who's on fire for the Lord. Do you want to be that person? Through the work of the Holy Spirit, twelve disciples turned the world upside down. God is still in the business of disciple making.

The lukewarm Laodicean church existed in a wealthy city, but Christ called them *"poor."* In a place known for its medical school and healing ointments for the eye, Jesus said they were *"blind."* In a town famous for its production of black wool, Christ saw them *"naked"* and in need of His white robes of righteousness. But He didn't leave them without hope. He said, *"Here I am! I stand at the door and knock. If anyone hears my voice and opens the door, I will come in and eat with him, and he with me"* (Rev. 3:20).

Often that verse is used to lead the unsaved to the Savior. It certainly is true that Jesus invites sinners to open their hearts' doors so that He may come in. But remember the context of this verse. Jesus was speaking to the lost in church. He was saying, *" 'I know your deeds.'* You are not what you need to be. Therefore, you don't do what you ought to do. You don't know how needy you really are. I'm standing at the door of your heart. Open the door. Repent of your self-satisfaction and self-sufficiency. What you really need is Me!"

Chapter Three

Holiness or Hypocrisy?

*"On the outside you appear to people as righteous but on the
inside you are full of hypocrisy and wickedness."*
—Matthew 23:28

*"What kind of people ought you to be?
You ought to live holy and godly lives."*
—2 Peter 3:11

G lancing around the hospital room, the middle-aged
man sighed heavily, his irritation apparent.

"I don't get it with you people. There's absolutely
nothing wrong with me!"

"Sir, I understand your impatience," the doctor responded kindly. "But you must trust me on this—you are
in serious need of medical attention. Whether you realize
it or not, you are very sick."

The man's face reddened as his anger intensified. He
started to lift himself off the examining table as two
nurses moved to restrain him.

"You people just don't understand! I feel fine. Leave
me alone!"

The doctor looked the man straight in the eyes and
said, "Sir, you must accept the facts. You have cancer.
You know that if it is left untreated, it will kill you." The
practitioner lowered his bifocals below eye level to gaze
sternly at the man. "Sir, you must face reality."

Aggravated, the man dropped back to the table and grunted. "You don't know what you're talking about. I'm going to live to be a hundred years old—at least!"

The doctor had seen this type of denial many times before. If patients couldn't recognize the symptoms of their disease, if they couldn't feel the pain or sense the urgency of the situation, then most refused to believe their diagnosis. Naively, they trusted in their own mortality.

Like this patient, many today deny that they need spiritual help. They refuse to think about their eternal futures. If they can't recognize the problem, they act like doubting Thomas. Reacting to the news that Jesus was alive, Thomas said, *"Unless I see the nail marks in his hands and put my finger where the nails were, and put my hand into his side, I will not believe it"* (John 20:25).

Eight days later, Christ appeared to the disciples again, but this time Thomas was with them. Jesus spoke directly to him and said, *"Put your finger here; see my hands. Reach out your hand and put it into my side. Stop doubting and believe"* (v. 27).

What an amazing story! Remember that Thomas was one of Jesus' disciples. He had witnessed miracle after miracle and had spent intimate time with the Master of the universe, yet he was still unable and unwilling to believe without seeing things with his own eyes.

The average churchgoer could be compared to a doubting Thomas—or to a dying patient in denial. I'm not talking about believers who have been washed in the blood, who are filled with the Spirit, and who are running the good race with faithful devotion. Instead, I'm talking about people who wear a badge of religiosity but refuse to examine the real conditions of their hearts. Although they go through the outward motions of being a Christian, they have never experienced a genuine conversion. They are like the people whom Jesus described as experts at judging others while ignoring their own faults. He said,

Why do you look at the speck of sawdust in your brother's eye and pay no attention to the plank in your own eye? How can you say to your brother, "Let me take the speck out of your eye," when all the time there is a plank in your own eye? (Matt. 7:3–4)

Jesus called these people hypocrites. The term comes from the Greek and means "actor." Back before modern methods of amplification were available, actors had to wear masks with small megaphones built into them. That way, their voices could be heard by the people sitting in the ancient amphitheaters. So a hypocrite is one who wears a mask. His life is like a house with false walls, two-way mirrors, and trap doors. Everyone can see his compromised lifestyle—everyone, that is, but him. A hypocrite is blinded by his own religious fervor, confident that God couldn't make it another day without him on His side. He is convinced that God's mercy will fall on him no matter what he does, thinks, or says.

Consider the similarities between hypocrisy and cancer:

- Both are often deadly.
- Many who suffer from these conditions either don't know it or refuse to admit it and seek appropriate treatment.
- Both are harmful. Cancer devastates the physical body, while hypocrisy destroys the spirit.
- A qualified individual can accurately diagnose both. Cancer can be identified by physicians; hypocrisy, by Spirit-filled Christians.
- Both require drastic measures to annihilate, and the remedies are not pleasant: chemotherapy causes sickness; repentance and cross-bearing cost your self-will.
- Appropriate treatments offer hope for the future.
- Both begin deep inside the body, starting so innocuously that they are practically undetectable, but if allowed to grow and fester, they can cause irreparable damage.

There is at least one notable difference, though, between hypocrisy and cancer. Cancer is limited to the body that it is destroying, but hypocrisy corrupts the person it infects as well as poisons those who come in contact with it. It's highly infectious and seeks to contaminate anybody who's drawn in by its seductiveness. Hypocrisy says, "Do as I say, not as I do." Hypocrisy results from a lukewarm heart that refuses to bow before its Creator.

Hypocrisy is one of the greatest tools the devil uses to deceive human beings. A hypocritical spirit is not selective in whom it infects. It does not limit its pollution to a certain age, gender, ethnicity, or social status.

The Lord's reaction to hypocrisy in the church is nothing short of astonishing. His harshest words were not for the woman caught in adultery, but for the hypocrite. His anger didn't flare against the stealing ways of the tax collectors as it did against hypocrites. When confronted with unbelief and wickedness, Jesus offered hope and forgiveness to those who truly repented. Hypocrisy, however, made His blood boil, so to speak. Look at this story He told about two servants.

> *Who then is the faithful and wise servant, whom the master has put in charge of the servants in his household to give them their food at the proper time? It will be good for that servant whose master finds him doing so when he returns. I tell you the truth, he will put him in charge of all his possessions. But suppose that servant is wicked and says to himself, "My master is staying away a long time," and he then begins to beat his fellow servants and to eat and drink with drunkards. The master of that servant will come on a day when he does not expect him and at an hour he is not aware of. He will cut him to pieces and assign him a place with the hypocrites, where there will be weeping and gnashing of teeth.* (Matt. 24:45–51)

Two types of servants are described here. The first is faithful, wise, and trustworthy. He provides for others and is blessed and content in carrying out the assignments that have been given to him—to supervise the servants in the house and provide food for them. His consistent obedience will lead to increased responsibilities, along with greater trust from his master.

The second servant is evil, irresponsible, and unreliable. He not only disregards his responsibilities, but he also begins to mistreat his fellow servants. He adopts the heathen ways of the world and takes up company with the wrong crowd. He's no longer concerned about his master's wishes but only about his own selfish desires. Since his master hasn't appeared for many years, he begins to believe that it no longer matters how he acts. He thinks that perhaps his master is dead. But when his master does return, the judgment that falls on this servant will be severe.

The difference between these individuals is phenomenal, yet both types are represented in the church today. One serves the Lord wholeheartedly, while the other follows his own evil flesh. But as we delve more closely into these verses, it becomes painfully clear that there aren't necessarily two servants in the Lord's mind, but one! We have a choice over which kind of servant we will be.

In the parable of the sower in Matthew 13, Jesus speaks of one who started the journey well but ended poorly.

> *The one who received the seed that fell on rocky places is the man who hears the word and at once receives it with joy. But since he has no root, he lasts only a short time. When trouble or persecution comes because of the word, he quickly falls away.* (vv. 20–21)

When a person responds to Christ's calling, the world sees a person who is excited about the Lord, who is witnessing about God's goodness, and who is walking the straight and narrow path to heaven; but if that person

consciously stumbles into evil and consistently refuses to repent, the world sees hypocrisy. The end result for unrepentant hypocrites is to be *"cut in two"* (Matt. 24:51 NKJV) and assigned to a place where there will *"be weeping and gnashing of teeth"* (v. 51). Does this sound like heaven? It doesn't require a Bible scholar to point out the tragedy in this parable. Jesus Christ still takes hypocrisy seriously and judges it harshly!

Consider these verses:

> *When a righteous man turns from his righteousness and does evil, and I put a stumbling block before him, he will die. Since you did not warn him, he will die for his sin. The righteous things he did will not be remembered, and I will hold you accountable for his blood.*
> (Ezek. 3:20)

> *I know your deeds; you have a reputation of being alive, but you are dead. Wake up! Strengthen what remains and is about to die, for I have not found your deeds complete in the sight of my God. Remember, therefore, what you have received and heard; obey it, and repent. But if you do not wake up, I will come like a thief, and you will not know at what time I will come to you. Yet you have a few people in Sardis who have not soiled their clothes. They will walk with me, dressed in white, for they are worthy. He who overcomes will, like them, be dressed in white. I will never blot out his name from the book of life, but will acknowledge his name before my Father and his angels.*
> (Rev. 3:1–5)

> *Blessed are those who do His commandments, that they may have the right to the tree of life, and may enter through the gates into the city. But outside are dogs and sorcerers and sexually immoral and murderers and idolaters, and **whoever loves and practices a lie**.*
> (Rev. 22:14–15 NKJV, emphasis added)

Hypocrites do not have the faith to obey God. Although true Christians may occasionally react hypocritically, they repent and ask God for forgiveness. On the other hand, hypocrites consistently act in this abhorrent way. Although they claim to be Christians, most are nothing more than imposters who serve the evil one—and they may not even know it. On Judgment Day, the Bible explicitly says that God will look at our faith-inspired works. Our works are the evidence of our faith. Hypocrites claim to have supernatural faith, yet their good works are strangely absent or few and far between. Their words and actions don't match up.

Rebecca's father watched his ten-year-old from the kitchen window. He noticed that she glanced over her shoulder before grabbing onto one of the branches of the oak tree. Trying to remain calm, he hurried outside.

"Rebecca!" he yelled, as he ran toward the old tree.

She was hanging upside down when the weak branch gave way, causing her to fall to the ground.

"Are you okay?" he called as he rushed to her side. "I told you not to climb that tree!"

Rebecca started crying as her father picked her up. The young girl angrily tucked her face into her father's chest and howled in protest.

"No, I'm not!"

Her father carried her to a chair on the deck and carefully sat her down. She didn't appear to be injured. He gently placed his hands on her shoulders and sighed. She refused to look at him as he spoke.

"How many times have I told you not to climb that tree? It's old, and its branches are weak."

She looked away for a moment, then turned to face her dad.

"I'm sorry, Dad. I didn't mean to. I won't do it again."

Her repentance appeared genuine, yet her father knew better. This was the *tenth* time this month he had caught her climbing that tree. He had tried talking to her, threatening her, even punishing her, yet nothing had worked.

"Rebecca, look at me!" he demanded in a tone she didn't like hearing. "You are not sorry, because if you were, you would obey."

She started to talk, but he placed his finger on her lips and shook his head.

"Not a word." He took a deep breath and continued. "You have lied to me, Rebecca. You *did* mean to climb that tree. If you didn't, you wouldn't have climbed it and fallen."

Rebecca didn't like to hear the truth, especially from her father.

"For the tenth time this month, you tell me you 'won't do it again.'"

Rebecca did her best to look sincere.

"I mean it this time, Dad. Really."

Sadly, her father said, "How can I trust you? By repeatedly disobeying, you've shown that you are not really sorry for what you've done and that you have no intention of listening to me and your mother."

"That's not true! I just made a mistake." She tilted her head and flashed a smile. "Cut me some slack, Dad."

Her empty words cut at her father. Rebecca turned toward the tree. It still looked inviting. As she glanced over at her neighbor's house, she saw her best friend Samantha and Samantha's mother sitting on their deck. They had had a clear view of what had taken place.

Samantha turned to her mother and asked, "Mom, how come Rebecca won't listen to her father? I thought she was a Christian."

Her mother sighed. She didn't have a good answer. She didn't know how to explain hypocrisy to her daughter.

Because obedience is not an option for Christians, the behavior of hypocrites confuses people. They wonder, "Doesn't God expect people to obey Him? If someone claims to love the Lord, then shouldn't he listen to Him? Shouldn't Christians trust that God knows best?"

Yet some Christians haven't grasped this critical truth: Christians are called to be pure—to be different from the world. Most hypocrites allow sin to reign in their lives. Their sins are not accidents; they are willful and often premeditated. This is a dangerous attitude that is addressed in Hebrews 10:26–27:

> *If we deliberately keep on sinning after we have re-ceived the knowledge of the truth, no sacrifice for sins is left, but only a fearful expectation of judgment and of raging fire that will consume the enemies of God.*

Don't get me wrong. People make mistakes, and Jesus forgives their transgressions. The primary purpose of the cross is to reconcile sinners to God through the forgive-ness of sins. But a hypocrite sits on the edge of a spiri-tual cliff, taking advantage of God's mercy and saying, "Oh, well, God forgives me." This passage in Hebrews blows a hole in the hypocrite's theology that says, "It doesn't matter what I do; I'm forgiven." Let's dig deeper into the truths of this passage.

Look at the first thought: *"Deliberately keep on sin-ning."* Hypocrites know they are sinning, yet they do it anyway. Most hypocrites try to battle their sin through their own power. They don't know how to tap into the unlimited, omnipotent power of the Holy Spirit. Romans 7:15 says, *"I do not understand what I do. For what I want to do I do not do, but what I hate I do."* Verse 25 continues, *"Thanks be to God—through Jesus Christ our Lord! So then, I myself in my mind am a slave to God's law, but in the sinful nature a slave to the law of sin."*

Some in the church point to these verses and con-clude that everybody who has ever made a "profession of faith" is going to heaven. The next verse dispels that line of reasoning. Romans 8:1 concludes, *"There is therefore now no condemnation to those who are in Christ Jesus, who do not walk according to the flesh, but according to*

the Spirit" (NKJV). Who is in Christ Jesus? Is it the hypocrite or the lukewarm professor of faith? No! Those people are walking *"according to the flesh."* There is condemnation for them, but not for those who are walking *"according to the Spirit."* Heaven-bound people are filled with the Holy Spirit, and it is that Spirit that cleanses them, changes them, and enables them to say no to the flesh and yes to Jesus.

The text from Hebrews 10 continues, *"No sacrifice for sins is left"* (v. 26). Jesus is our Sacrificial Lamb. Without His death on the cross—His complete sacrifice of Himself—there could be no hope of heaven for mortals. Hypocrites who willfully sin and consistently live *"according to the flesh"* cannot claim Jesus as the Forgiver of their sins because *"no sacrifice for sins is left."* Of course, they can repent and begin to walk *"according to the Spirit,"* but many never respond to the Holy Spirit's calling. The truth of this verse must be taken with utmost seriousness. Too many lost in church today never grasp the need for holiness or the horror of hypocrisy.

Those who fear God do not fall into this trap, though. Consider Solomon's life for a moment. Solomon backslid big-time! In his early years, he was on fire for God, but as the years wore on, his strong faith wilted. After trying every form of evil pleasure to fulfill himself, he came to this conclusion in Ecclesiastes 12:13–14:

> *Here is the conclusion of the matter: Fear God and keep his commandments, for this is the whole duty of man. For God will bring every deed into judgment, including every hidden thing, whether it is good or evil.*

Thank God Solomon came to his senses and renewed his faith. He repented of his evil and came to God with a new sense of love for his Creator.

Our text from Hebrews 10 tells us what is left for the unrepentant hypocrite: *"a fearful expectation of judgment"*

(v. 27). Hypocrites often fear death because deep inside, they know something is dreadfully wrong. If lost church-goers were polled about their chances of going to heaven, many would answer something like this.

- I have a really good shot at it. Basically, I'm a good person.
- I'm almost certain I'll make it.
- I'll take my chances. I'm as good as the next guy.

Many in the church are not assured of their salvation. A born-again Christian must be assured that he is born into the family of God, washed clean by the blood, and on his way to eternal glory with God. Others would prefer to extend their flesh-filled lives on earth for as long as possible. They'd rather put off making a decision for Christ. They've heard occasional messages on righteousness, holiness, hell, and other subjects not too popular today, but they tuck these warnings away without truly considering the implications for their souls. They do not understand what it means to fear God.

The last part of the Hebrews text warns of a *"raging fire that will consume the enemies of God"* (v. 27). These words paint a picture of hell swallowing up anything or anyone not of God. It's not a pleasant picture, but it is the truth.

Many hypocrites and lukewarm Christians are at enmity with God. In other words, they are adversaries of God because of their chosen lifestyles. Jesus Christ becomes indignant with people who say one thing and do another.

Let's take a look at how Jesus exposed the hypocrisy of the religious elders of that time. It is no wonder they plotted to kill Him after He uncovered their true natures. Their attitudes were similar to some in the church today who say,

- How dare He mess with my traditions. I'm not going to change!

- We've done it this way for as long as I can remember.
- What I do is not as important as what I believe.
- God is on my side no matter what I do.
- You're not going to change my mind. What I believe is what I believe!
- You don't understand, brother. God forgives me of whatever I do. That's what the cross is for.

Before you continue with this chapter, please read the twenty-third chapter of Matthew prayerfully. Read it several times. Ask for God's assistance in understanding His Word, and pray for His conviction on any area of your life that needs correction.

Now, let's begin by looking at Matthew 23:2: *"The teachers of the law and the Pharisees sit in Moses' seat."* These religious hypocrites held high offices and used their influential positions to impose their interpretations of Scripture on others. Beware of false prophets and preachers who give only part of the truth. Flee from them as if running from a ravenous wolf. Some ministers use their platforms to endorse and promote their own form of Christianity. Remember, an individual's title or circle of influence does not always translate into a measure of his godliness. Christians, beware! Rely primarily on Jesus Christ and His Holy Scriptures to transform and mold you, not someone's fancy words. Please don't misunderstand. I'm not suggesting that you stay away from church or that you be unmoved by the words of God's representative behind the pulpit. I am saying that you must study the Word of God for yourself; make sure the Bible supports what you are hearing preached.

Verse 4 says, *"They tie up heavy loads and put them on men's shoulders, but they themselves are not willing to lift a finger to move them."* Beware of legalistic hypocrisy. Hypocrites love to criticize and look down on others. They create dozens of man-made rules—some good, some bad—but refuse to show people how to obey them. They bog people down with rules without showing them the true power behind obedience: the Holy Spirit. The *New Living Translation* puts this verse right where we live. It says, *"They crush you with impossible religious demands and never lift a finger to help ease the burden."* Hypocrites often appear to be very religious, while imposing their moral codes onto others. Their form of religion weighs people down instead of lifting them up. The grace of God and the freedom we have in Christ is absent from their theology.

"Everything they do is done for men to see" (v. 5). For the born-again Christian, motivation and attitude are incredibly important. Hypocrites are essentially motivated by pride. They try to catch the eye of men instead of seeking the attention of God. Although many are moral people, they do their good works in order to receive the praise of men. Even worse, they add to the Word of God, heaping curses upon themselves and those who listen to them. (See Revelation 22:18.) Attitude is everything.

> When [Jesus] was in the house, he asked them, "What were you arguing about on the road?" But they kept quiet because on the way they had argued about who was the greatest. Sitting down, Jesus called the Twelve and said, "If anyone wants to be first, he must be the very last, and the servant of all."   (Mark 9:33–35)

The disciples were more concerned with what men thought of them than what God thought. They feared men more than God. Proverbs 29:25 rebukes this attitude. It says, *"Fear of man will prove to be a snare, but whoever trusts in the LORD is kept safe."* Our motivation for doing good and obeying God should be our love, respect, and fear of God. Any other impetus for good works is carnal, prideful, and dangerous.

"Woe to you, teachers of the law and Pharisees, you hypocrites! You shut the kingdom of heaven in men's faces. You yourselves do not enter, nor will you let those enter who are trying to" (v. 13). Although an occasional

act of hypocrisy does not automatically disqualify a person from heaven, a Christian cannot maintain his relationship with the Lord and practice hypocrisy on a regular basis. With the help of the Holy Spirit, we can rid ourselves of this *"sin that so easily entangles"* (Heb. 12:1).

Another hideous side of hypocrisy is described in the second part of Matthew 23:13. Those who are trying to make it to heaven, those who are seeking to know God in a personal way and obey His commands, are often led down the wrong path by hypocrites. Many of these lost sheep looking for their home will never find it because of these wolves dressed in sheep's clothing. Consider Matthew 18:6: *"But if anyone causes one of these little ones who believe in me to sin, it would be better for him to have a large millstone hung around his neck and to be drowned in the depths of the sea."* This is a type of spiritual kidnapping, and the punishment is severe, everlasting, and proper. Hypocrites are no closer to God than a murderer on death row. Steer clear of them because their lies could blow up in your face like land mines, spreading spiritual shrapnel that can maim and kill.

As we continue to look at the truths in Matthew 23, we see this warning:

> *Woe to you, teachers of the law and Pharisees, you hypocrites! You give a tenth of your spices—mint, dill and cummin. But you have neglected the more important matters of the law—justice, mercy and faithfulness. You should have practiced the latter, without neglecting the former.* (v. 23)

The *New Living Translation* begins this verse with these words: *"How terrible it will be for you."* A hypocrite's eternal future is a frightening thing to contemplate. Jesus uncovered their pretentiousness—their penchant for focusing on the minute while ignoring the momentous. They would give a tenth of their increase—including a tithe on their spices—yet would turn around and neglect the more significant aspects of the law. Their faith was not in God, but in their own self-imposed, man-made morality. Yes, it made them feel good to be religious, but feelings aren't enough to get one into heaven. There was no justice, love, or mercy in their hearts for anyone who disagreed with their religion; as a result, they killed Jesus. Jesus wasn't telling people not to tithe, but to love God and their fellowmen while giving generously to the church and those in need.

Self-righteousness not only destroys the one who practices it but also damages others. Consider this story of one family.

Margaret stormed into the living room and glared at her husband Joe, who was sprawled across the couch. He was enjoying some popcorn while he watched the adventure movie he had rented.

"What are you doing?" Her tone was caustic and demeaning.

Joe kept his eyes glued to the screen as he nonchalantly responded.

"I'm watching a movie. What are you doing? On another witch-hunt?"

Margaret was incensed by his response. She went to church every Sunday and claimed to be a Christian. Joe, however, didn't think he needed God since he felt as if he lived with the devil. Margaret's religious demands were more than he could take.

"I can't believe you brought that movie into this house!" she fumed. Their three kids, who were trying to fall asleep, could hear her from their beds. "I told you nothing but G-rated movies in my house!" Margaret was possessed with anger. "You are inviting demons in this house and are corrupting our kids!"

Joe rolled his eyes as he turned to meet his wife's angry face. "Calm down. It's just PG-13."

Margaret stomped out of the room. Grabbing her Bible from the kitchen counter, she quickly opened it to

Revelation 21 and began to read in her loudest voice: *"But the cowardly, the unbelieving, the vile, the murderers."* The pitch and intensity of her voice increased with each word. *"The sexually immoral, those who practice magic arts, the idolaters and all liars—their place will be in the fiery lake of burning sulfur. This is the second death."*

So consumed by her anger, Margaret didn't hear her five-year-old start to cry. The child didn't understand what her mommy was yelling about, but her mother's anger was all too familiar. The oldest child, ten-year-old Michael, blankly stared at the ceiling. He had stopped praying to God months ago, unable to reconcile his mother's behavior with what he had been taught in Sunday school. The middle child, Blake, slid out of bed and dropped to his knees. He loved Jesus and prayed, "Please help Daddy, and make Mommy nice."

I hope you won't misunderstand the point of this story. Many movies are totally unacceptable for Christians to watch, but Margaret was trying to change the morals of her husband before his heart had been changed by the Lord. Sadly, she was not practicing love, peace, or mercy, but her own version of morality, which was devoid of the prompting of the Spirit. Everybody could see the devil of hypocrisy in her life—everybody, that is, but her. Think what could have happened if she had followed the biblical advice found in 1 Peter 3:1–2:

> *Wives, in the same way be submissive to your husbands so that, if any of them do not believe the word, they may be won over without words by the behavior of their wives, when they see the purity and reverence of your lives.*

Matthew 23 continues warning those who are focused on surface issues instead of on matters of the heart. It reads:

Woe to you, teachers of the law and Pharisees, you hypo-
crites! You clean the outside of the cup and dish, but in-
side they are full of greed and self-indulgence. Blind
Pharisee! First clean the inside of the cup and dish, and
then the outside also will be clean.   (Matt. 23:25–26)

Imagine you're seated in one of the finest restaurants
in town. A musician strolls from table to table, creating
heavenly melodies from his violin. Waiters are hand-
somely dressed in tuxedoes, the walls are lined with
tasteful art, and the soothing sounds of a waterfall me-
andering through a rock garden enhance the romantic
atmosphere. A waiter approaches your table.

"Good evening," he says in a smooth, pleasing tone.
"May I offer you something to drink?"

You smile and answer, "Yes, thank you. May we have
two cups of coffee?"

"Of course. I'll bring them right away." He expertly
places a napkin on your spouse's lap, then does the same
for you. As he walks away, you gaze into your wife's eyes.
You both know this is going to be a memorable evening.

A few minutes pass before the waiter returns with a
silver coffeepot and two sparkling porcelain cups. He
places the coffeepot on the table, then gently maneuvers
the cups onto their saucers. Before he can lift the pot of
coffee to pour it, you notice something inside your cup.
You quickly tilt the shining cup toward you. You can't
believe what you are seeing. The sight makes you sick.
The waiter has seen it, too, but he doesn't seem bothered; in fact, he's still ready to pour the coffee into the
cup. You look at him in astonishment.

"What seems to be the problem?" he asks, slightly
annoyed by your lack of civility.

You glance at the cups once more before turning toward the waiter.

"Don't you see the filth inside these cups? They look
like they haven't been washed in years."

The waiter picks up the cups from the table and looks into them. A second later he places them back on the saucers.

"They look fine to me. Did you notice how clean the outside is?"

Wanting to avoid any further embarrassment, your spouse touches your arm and whispers, "Let's just get out of here."

This story may appear to be absurd on the surface. What fancy restaurant wouldn't wash the inside of its cups? Yet too many people—some who attend church regularly—live their lives concerned only with outward appearances.

In this story, any coffee poured into the grimy cups would instantly be polluted by the filth inside. Drinking from the dirty cup could cause sickness. Likewise, how illogical it is for a person to try to clean up the outside while ignoring what's inside. When our hearts are dirty and controlled by the world's lusts, they can make us sick spiritually and physically. Even sugarcoated poison is dangerous. No matter how inviting the outside is, the contamination on the inside will kill. God wants to transform our lives from the inside out. Many lost in church are busily keeping the outside of their cups clean while ignoring the inside altogether. Only clean hearts washed by the blood of Christ will be allowed in heaven.

We can wash the inside of our cups. However, we can't become holy on our own. We must come to the cross and ask for the power of the Holy Spirit to cleanse and indwell us. Remember, what's on the inside will eventually be revealed for the world to see. Hypocrites may fool themselves into believing they are good enough for heaven, but 1 Timothy warns:

The sins of some men are obvious, reaching the place of judgment ahead of them; the sins of others trail behind

*them. In the same way, good deeds are obvious, and
even those that are not cannot be hidden.*

(1 Tim. 5:24–25)

Returning to Matthew 23, we read Jesus' condemnation of hypocrites: *"You snakes! You brood of vipers! How
will you escape being condemned to hell?"* (v. 33). Let's
get real for a moment. Let's look at hypocrisy through the
righteous eyes of Jesus Christ. He confronted the most
"religious" people on the face of the earth and called
them *"snakes"* and *"vipers."* He said they were on their
way to hell. His judgment cannot be misinterpreted.

It's time to remember that Satan is a serpent. Although he may appear as a sheep, he's a wolf who will
drag his victims to hell. Don't be misled by his tactics.
Are you consumed by what others think of you? Are you
tired of wearing a mask that hides the real you? Are you
willing to have your heart exposed to God's light? Then
pray as David did, *"Search me, O God, and know my
heart....See if there is any offensive way in me"* (Ps.
139:23–24).

Jesus calls hypocrites to set aside their pretension of
religion and allow Him to perform radical surgery on
their hearts. His scalpel will remove any contamination
and bring healing and wholeness. Allow the Great Physician to examine your heart today. Only He can transform
hypocrisy into holiness.

Chapter Four

Pursuing the Giver or the Gift?

"Where your treasure is, there your heart will be also."
—Matthew 6:21

If Jesus Christ were to come to your house for a heart-to-heart conversation with your family, what would you talk about? Most of us would stick with safe topics, such as these:

- The meaning of certain Scriptures
- God's love for you and your love for Him
- Missionaries and their good works
- What heaven looks like
- Our struggles, hopes, and desires

It would be a spiritual love feast. Imagine, then, that in the midst of this conversation, the Lord asks you a simple yet powerful question: "You say you love Me. Then why do you use your money as if it were your own?"

Suddenly, you feel as if a cannonball has plowed through you. You take a deep gulp and try to speak, but you can't. You know that *He knows*! For years you've acted as if He didn't see the way you spent your money, the way you ignored His commands to tithe and to give offerings. You pretended He was unaware of your pride and tight control over your material possessions. Now, you feel like a deer caught in the headlights of an eighteen-wheeler.

The world is consumed with the desire to get rich. From lotteries to pyramid schemes to working twelve- and fourteen-hour days, we want to "get ahead." We want to keep up with the Joneses, we want a more promising future for our children, and we want the latest gadgets. When is enough, enough? Where does God fit in your finances?

Pretend that it's the year 1453. You're a poor peasant in a vast kingdom ruled by a powerful king. Yesterday, royal messengers arrived at your door with an invitation to the castle. You can't sleep all night as you ponder your fate. The king's request seems friendly enough, yet your imagination muddies your joy. You worry, *What if I have done something to displease him?*

Morning finally arrives, and you make the arduous trip to the palace. On the way, you rehearse possible answers to the questions the king may ask. As you approach the castle entrance, your heart flutters. You can't believe it. The king has invited you into his throne room! It's the greatest thrill of your life. Few are invited into the castle; fewer yet are allowed into his private quarters.

Minutes later, you are on your knees before King Phillip. He looks joyful—a good sign, you think.

"I have summoned you today for a noble task."

You swallow hard as the king's eyes pierce you.

"I am giving you two tons of gold."

Your jaw drops. You try to say, "Thank you," but no words will come out.

"This is my money I'm granting to you. I expect a full accounting of every transaction you make. Is that clear?"

You nod your head. You can't believe this is happening.

"You will use this gold in my best interests, not your own. In effect, you are my agent. Are you sure you understand?"

The king's words bounce off you. You're now a multi-millionaire! You shake your head yes, without really comprehending what he is saying. Dozens of trumpets blare as you exit the castle with several of the king's men behind you, pushing carts filled with gold nuggets. Once you reach your home and the king's servants leave, you shout, "Hallelujah, I'm rich!"

A year later, you are sitting in your new mansion, which has been custom-built to your specifications. Several dozen servants are at your beck and call, responding to your most trivial whim. You have everything your heart desires, but you also have a major problem: You've spent all the gold. You find it strange that you haven't heard from your friend, the king. You decide to pay him a visit today in order to...replenish your coffers.

You approach the castle with your servants carrying you in your gem-adorned cart. You want to impress everyone. The guards at the gate see you and immediately blow the trumpets. As you enter the castle, pride wells up inside you. You don't have an invitation, but you figure it doesn't matter. The king and you are close, very close.

King Phillip says nothing as you approach his throne. His face reveals no emotion as you order your servants to stop. You catch the king's eye and wink. Suddenly, lightning flashes from his eyes. He grips the arms of his throne.

"What are you doing here?" he thunders.

You freeze. Your lips move, but nothing comes out.

"You come into *my house* as if you were the king. Who do you think you are?"

"I...I thought we were...were friends," you stutter.

"You are my friend if you respect me. You are my friend if you obey me. You are my friend if you take care of my subjects. Have you done these things? Do you have an accounting of all the gold I gave you?"

You close your eyes and wish for a miracle. Maybe this isn't happening; maybe you're having a nightmare. You wish that you'd never seen that gold. You hope for mercy, but expect judgment.

It's clear that the peasant in this story is foolish. He wastes the king's money and then has the gall to ask for more. What was his motivation for spending the gold as he did? Why did he squander the king's treasure? What should the king do to him? Did this man really love and respect his king?

I believe the point of this story is all too common among churchgoers today. Many say—by their actions, if not by their words—that the money they have belongs to them, not God. Obviously, the peasant in the story was unwise to waste the king's money on worldly pleasures. Many in the church do this same thing today. Doesn't the money in your pocket belong to King Jesus? How many say, "We can't afford to tithe, let alone give offerings"? Yet they do afford—

- new cars every few years
- a couple of vacations annually
- dinners in nice restaurants
- computers with the latest upgrades
- new televisions with larger screens
- credit card balances with outrageous interest charges

Some may think, "Wait a minute. You're sounding awfully legalistic." These comments might be legalistic if a family were already giving to the Lord according to the Spirit's leading. When you obey Jesus with your wallet, then you have freedom to spend the excess the way you desire because God controls your desires. I'm not suggesting that God wants us to live in poverty. But if money is your god, or if it has the potential to be a stumbling block spiritually, it would be better to be poor financially but rich spiritually.

Jesus blesses those who obey Him; often, but not always, He blesses them financially as well as spiritually. If people aren't obeying Him and giving generously, however, then the complaint that "tithing is an Old Testament concept and not applicable to the church today" is a thinly veiled excuse to spend money the way they want to spend it—without any consideration for God's plan.

The peasant's attitude is quite astounding. He completely disregards the king's commands, yet he thinks the two of them are buddies. This arrogant attitude is rampant in many church circles today. Some blatantly disobey the Lord with their finances but still expect God's blessings. Many are filled with a form of religious pride, thinking God owes them something for their service to Him. Like this foolish man, they are so consumed with the things of the world that they are blinded to the things of the kingdom. Scripture repeatedly reminds us to "open our eyes" to spiritual truths. A person cannot love God and ignore His commands concerning money. God's Word clearly says,

> Do not love the world or the things in the world. If anyone loves the world, the love of the Father is not in him.
> (1 John 2:15 NKJV)

Many in the church can quote this verse without ever considering its meaning. What does it mean to *"love the world"* and *"the things in the world"*? Practically everything in this world costs money. One could almost use the words *world* and *money* interchangeably in this verse. "Do not love money or the things money can buy. If anyone loves money, the love of the Father is not in him." Does the Bible support such an interpretation? First Timothy 6:9–11 says,

> But those who desire to be rich fall into temptation and a snare, and into many foolish and harmful lusts which drown men in destruction and perdition. For the love of money is a root of all kinds of evil, for which some have strayed from the faith in their greediness, and pierced themselves through with many sorrows. But you, O man of God, flee these things and pursue righteousness, godliness, faith, love, patience, gentleness. (NKJV)

71

Notice some of the words used in this passage: *"snare," "foolish and harmful lusts," "destruction and perdition," "greediness," "pierced," "sorrows."* Do these descriptions paint a picture of a Spirit-filled Christian? Although some churchgoers act as if God's grace and mercy will excuse or blink at all sin, Ephesians 5:5 tells us otherwise: *"For of this you can be sure: No immoral, impure or **greedy person**—such a man is an idolater—has any inheritance in the kingdom of Christ and of God"* (emphasis added).

Without an *"inheritance in the kingdom,"* a person is not a child of God and will *not* go to heaven. I believe we are living in the end times. We know from Scripture that as we approach the Age of the Antichrist, the devil's powers of deception will grow exponentially. And there is a great deception today among church folks concerning the biblical principles of managing finances. The Bible warns,

> *Let no one deceive you with empty words, for because of such things* [impurity, immorality, greed, love of the world] *God's wrath comes on those who are disobedient. Therefore do not be partakers with them. For you were once darkness, but now you are light in the Lord. Live as children of light.* (Eph. 5:6–8)

These verses point to one of the greatest travesties in the church. Although it is difficult to gather hard facts on this subject, here are two observations that are supported by my own experience and that of many others in ministry:

- Fifty to eighty percent of those sitting in the pews today do not have a vital relationship with the Lord.
- Twenty percent of the people do eighty percent of the giving.

Let's examine the numbers for a moment. Assume that 80 percent in the church do not have a real walk with God, evidenced by spiritual fruit, personal holiness, and an intense desire to please the Lord. After all, these are the attributes of a born-again Christian. Simply making a profession of faith or praying at the altar alone is not enough. Don't get me wrong; professing your faith, having the humility to stand in front of the church and ask God for forgiveness, is an important step to take, but if fruit doesn't follow, then something is drastically wrong.

Think about it. If only 20 percent of churchgoers are truly saved, it's those 20 percent who do most of the giving! Wow! Could the picture be any clearer? *Born-again Christians obey God's commandments on giving.* The other 80 percent either toss a small amount God's way—money that they won't miss or won't cause them any "hardship"—or they don't give anything at all. Don't misunderstand. One cannot buy his way into God's kingdom. Salvation can come only through accepting the Lord's gift of forgiveness. Giving does not save you—but giving is an evidence of your salvation. A person who loves God puts his money where his faith is!

Were you taught as a child never to discuss religion or politics at the dinner table? An adaptation of that principle has found its way into the lukewarm church: One should never discuss money, but it's fine to—

- Talk about God's love.
- Tell about His patience.
- Encourage people so they can make it through the day.
- Preach sermons that make everyone feel good.

Just don't tell anyone how to spend his money!

Christianity is not a difficult concept to grasp. It works like this: Confess your sins to God, and He cleanses you. Because your heart and mind are renewed by His grace, you make new decisions. *These decisions are in obedience to God's Word.*

Christians put their money where their faith is because their lives are controlled by their transformed hearts and minds. What's in the heart comes out of the mouth. What's in the heart also comes out in the percentage of your income that you give back to God. Believers in Christ know who God is and what He expects.

Malachi records a time when the people of Israel did not understand the character of God or what He expected of His people. Listen carefully to the Lord's words:

> *"Ever since the time of your forefathers you have turned away from my decrees and have not kept them. Return to me, and I will return to you," says the LORD Almighty. "But you ask, 'How are we to return?' Will a man rob God? Yet you rob me. But you ask, 'How do we rob you?' In tithes and offerings. You are under a curse—the whole nation of you—because you are robbing me. Bring the whole tithe into the storehouse, that there may be food in my house. Test me in this," says the LORD Almighty, "and see if I will not throw open the floodgates of heaven and pour out so much blessing that you will not have room enough for it."* (Mal. 3:7–10)

During Malachi's day, the people didn't understand why God was upset with them. God told them to return to Him, yet they seemed confused by His rebuke. After all, they were God's chosen people. They thought that nothing could separate them from His love and that God accepted them for who they were. This dangerous mindset is alive and well today. Like a plague, this simplistic theology has swept across much of the globe. It highlights one part of God's character while conveniently ignoring the rest. In reality, the people of Malachi's day did understand what God expected, but they willfully chose to ignore it.

God would be denying who He is, His very essence, if He looked the other way at today's lust for money. This form of idolatry is especially dangerous because wealth often pushes God out of people's lives. Jesus Christ becomes another convenience to be used for selfish purposes. When obedience hurts, they refuse to obey. When obedience is easy, they smile and tell themselves what good people they are. One of the hardest things to do is to part with our hard-earned money. But consider this indisputable fact: Without God, we couldn't make money. God gives us eyes to see, ears to hear, health to work, and minds to think.

When people truly believe that God gives them the ability to produce wealth, they will honor Him with their money. How thankful to God are you for the ability that He has blessed you with to be able to work? Those who love their money and the things it buys keep it for themselves. Does God's rebuke—"You rob me!"—apply to you?

Robbery is a serious crime. Some countries put thieves away for months, while others incarcerate them for years. In some places, a thief is punished by having his hand cut off. If he is caught stealing again, he loses the other hand as well! Likewise, God takes the theft of His possessions seriously. He will not return to a thief's house until that thief repents. God says, *"Return to me, and I will return to you"* (Mal. 3:7). God will get what belongs to Him. Will we give it willingly with a cheerful heart, or will He remove His blessings and protection from us?

Think about these examples:

- Appliances in your house don't have their normal life span. Could God extend their time of usage?
- You have an insatiable desire to spend money and accumulate possessions. Could God remove that unhealthy desire?
- You ask for a raise, but your boss laughs in your face. Could God influence your boss's decision?

Some like to think of God as the "Big Guy" in heaven who occasionally intervenes in their lives. That is the

furthest thing from the truth! God has every hair on our heads numbered (Matt. 10:30). If allowed, He wants to be involved in every aspect of our lives. Consider the significance of Malachi 3:11. God says that if Israel will obey Him in their giving, He *"will rebuke the devourer for* [their] *sakes, so that he will not destroy the fruit of* [their] *ground, nor shall the vine fail to bear fruit for* [them] *in the field"* (nkjv). In other words, God will bless you if you obey Him.

Many churches are in financial trouble today. Granted, some are fiscally irresponsible because of unwise leadership, while others spend money extravagantly and call it "exercising their faith." Some are more concerned with big buildings and fancy theatrics than doing God's work. But, in many cases, churches today have a majority of their congregation who are deep in sin. These so-called religious folks ignore God's commands to give of themselves and their money. Then they wonder why their church can't pay the electric bill, replace that twenty-year-old carpet, help feed the poor, or set up programs designed to reach their neighborhoods for Christ. Malachi 3:10 states, *"'Bring the whole tithe into the storehouse, that there may be food in my house. Test me in this,' says the Lord Almighty."* Do you see what God is saying? Give to Him, and He will take that money and empower His church with programs to feed and house the poor and downcast.

Have you ever wondered why the government is doing the work of the church? Is it really the government's role to take care of those in trouble? In America, the 1960s was a time of dramatic social change, not all of it for good. During this time, the church abdicated its God-given role to help the needy. The government was more than happy to rush into this vacuum of despair and poverty and create constituents who relied on its programs to provide for their needs. History teaches us to be wary of government because it often wants to replace God in people's hearts and minds. If the sleeping church would wake up, repent, be filled with the Holy Spirit, and give to God His rightful share, then millions would see the compassion and caring of these fire-filled Christians and would give their hearts to the Lord. Revival would explode with a power from heaven few have ever seen. If only we would trust God with all our hearts, all our minds, all our souls, and all our money! Obedience is the golden key that will unlock the door to revival.

God demands our obedience, yet He promises vast blessings for our cooperation. Malachi 3:10 records God's promise: "'Test me in this,' says the LORD Almighty, 'and see if I will not throw open the floodgates of heaven and pour out so much blessing that you will not have room enough for it.'" In other words, God is saying, "Test Me. Try My way for yourself. Give it a shot, and you won't be disappointed!"

He knows how difficult it is for us to trust Him with our finances, yet He expects it no matter what our circumstances are. Some people say, "I have a legitimate reason for not giving, and God understands." The Bible says, *"Give, and it will be given to you"* (Luke 6:38). Your responsibility to give is not conditional on the amount in your bank account. Excuses for sinning won't hold up on Judgment Day. God will undoubtedly hear these words from many in the church:

- I couldn't afford to tithe.
- I didn't know it was that important.
- I thought the church was being greedy.
- The pastor talked too much about giving.
- My taxes helped to care for the underprivileged.
- I did give something when I could afford it.
- I was giving—to my responsibilities, my spouse, and my kids.
- I thought that 10 percent was a legalistic number.
- I didn't like the way the church was being run, so I wasn't going to support it.
- You just don't understand. I had a lot of debt, so it was impossible to give to the church.

Jesus Christ is long-suffering; His forgiveness is immeasurable, but on Judgment Day, many if not most who make these declarations will hear these words from our Lord: *"Woe to you who are rich, for you have already received your comfort"* (Luke 6:24).

Bill had been a deacon in his church for nearly twenty years, but he gave up that church position when he was promoted to vice president of his company. He was doing his best to ignore the correlation between his success in business and his failure as a husband, father, and Christian. The last thing he wanted was to hear what his wife Barbara had to say.

"I've done everything you've asked of me," his wife said softly. Her hands trembled as she pushed her hair back from her face. "I've been a loving, submissive wife, and I've prayed faithfully for you." Sadness turned to frustration as her eyes met his. "Yet you still won't admit the truth!"

Bill's angry response was anything but righteous.

"I'm sick and tired of your preaching. God accepts me for who I am—why won't you?"

Barbara reached for his hand, hoping to diffuse his defensiveness, but he pulled away. Still, she wasn't going to let him manipulate her or the situation this time.

"Bill, you know when this started." Instantly, he looked away. "Once you were promoted, your priorities changed." She grabbed a tissue and wiped her nose. As she looked at her husband, she mourned the changes in him. He had been so alive once, so full of joy and the Spirit, but now his eyes revealed a wasteland. "Bill, what's happened to you? You hardly go to church anymore. You've all but stopped giving of your time and your money."

She wanted to say more, but the Spirit led her to stop. Bill continued to act as if she were invisible, while he delayed answering.

Finally, he mumbled, "Well, maybe I've made a few mistakes." His voice grew louder. "But it doesn't mean you have to crucify me!"

Barbara prayed for a miracle—any kind of break-through that would bring peace to her family again. She longed to have her husband back—the man who read the Bible with her, who cheerfully gave to those in need, who served God and the church, and who treated her as if she was something special, a gift from their Father in heaven. She noticed that he was deep in thought.

"Do you really think it was the promotion?"

Barbara smiled, relieved.

"Yes, honey, I do. Once you got that position, you immediately went out and bought that boat. Then, since you work six days a week, night and day, you said that Sunday was the only time you could enjoy it." He glanced at her as she continued. "You started by going to the lake after church. Then you realized you didn't have time to do what you wanted to do." Barbara reached for his hand, and this time he didn't pull back. "Ever since the kids finished college, you've taken all the extra money and spent it on toys. You bought the boat, the sports car, and then that expensive camera. Don't you see the pattern?"

Bill's eyes glazed with tears. The Holy Spirit was speaking to him.

"Bill, this extra money we've had has done something to you that I don't like. You seem more interested in all your stuff than in me, the kids, the church, or even God!"

Barbara tried to read what he was thinking. This was the second time this month that she had confronted him about his lifestyle. The first time had ended with his denials and angry explosions.

Bill's thoughts were spinning. He didn't want to face up to his sin or the spiraling downward course of his spiritual life.

"I see what you're saying." Just as Barbara's hopes were rising, his voice took on a cruel tone. "You're upset because I'm starting to live life and enjoy it! You're just jealous because you're stuck in the same rut. This is all about you!" Barbara sobbed as she saw what was happening to the man she loved.

"No...no...no. I don't care about that stuff. I just want my husband back."

In disgust, Bill got up and headed toward the front door. Sarcastically, he said, "Don't wait up for me. I'm going fishing with my friends. Oh, what a sinner I am!"

His cynicism cut through Barbara. Her body rocked slowly back and forth as she thought about their future. She hated all the extra money. Bill's love of it was robbing her family and their future.

Tragedies of this sort are being played out across the globe as materialism and the love of money ensnare families in deceit and idolatry. The issue is one of trust. Do we trust God enough to give Him what He deserves, or do we do our own thing to our own demise? God's Word says, *"For where your treasure is, there your heart will be also"* (Matt. 6:21); and *"You cannot serve both God and Money"* (v. 24).

What caused Bill to pursue pleasure? Did his love for money suddenly appear out of thin air? Why was he putting his worldly treasures above God, the church, and his wife? The answer lies deep in the human heart. It's a sin so subtle and cleverly disguised by the enemy that most never notice it until it has blossomed like a poisonous flower. I'm speaking of pride. Think about it for a moment. Pride tells us:

- God doesn't really understand my situation.
- God demands more than I can afford.
- Tithing and all this giving stuff is outdated.
- God doesn't want to micromanage my life.
- I don't love money. I just enjoy nice things.
- God wants me to be happy.

After Jesus taught on wealth in Matthew 6, He concluded with this command:

But seek first the kingdom of God and His righteousness, and all these things shall be added to you. Therefore do not worry about tomorrow, for tomorrow will worry about its own things. (Matt. 6:33–34 NKJV)

Many in the church today want the best for their spouses and their children. They want strong relationships, a pure walk with God, and a life dedicated to Jesus. Because habits and sins from their unsaved days are forgiven and forgotten, the last stronghold the enemy can attack is in the area of money. Only the mighty hand of God can protect us from the bondage of loving money.

How do we become vulnerable to temptation in this area? Simply put, by not seeking God. Jesus concluded His speech on money by telling the church to actively pursue Him and His righteousness. I believe if you apply the principles that follow, God will turn your life upside down and then right side up. He will bless you in ways that are unimaginable.

- Commit to studying the Bible daily; this is how we come to know God intimately.
- Through prayer, ask God to give you the desires of His heart, not yours; this is how God purges us of our rebellious natures.
- Commit to purity in all areas of your life. Ask for His grace and help for just one hour at a time. At the end of that hour, pray for His strength to remain pure through the next hour. Continue to pray that way throughout the day.
- Ask Jesus to purge any worry from your heart. Many refuse to trust God with their finances because they can't "see" how it will all work out at the end of each month's billing cycle.
- Ask God to help you stop thinking about the things of this world—bills, college tuition, food, clothing, and anything else that's stealing your peace and joy in the Lord.

God wants a commitment from us, not to be perfect through our own efforts, but to seek Him so that He can make us perfect through His grace. Every one of the above suggestions requires God's power to accomplish. God will honor our prayers when they are focused on our spiritual growth. Be assured that He will answer your pleas not to allow wealth to hinder your relationship with Him. But you must seek Him with all your might first. Remember the promises in Matthew 7:7:

> *Ask and it will be given to you; seek and you will find; knock and the door will be opened to you. For everyone who asks receives; he who seeks finds; and to him who knocks, the door will be opened.*

Our Lord often says no to prayers that are prayed selfishly or are out of His will. But He will answer prayers that bring us closer to Him. We know that our growing relationship with the Master is His priority.

"Mom, come on! Give it to me, now!" bellowed little Tommy, jumping around like a disoriented kangaroo.

Angela, Tommy's mother, sat motionless on the living room couch. She had noticed Tommy's attitude toward his allowance grow increasingly unhealthy in the past several months.

"Tommy, calm down and sit beside me." Her tone told him she meant business. The seven-year-old boy plopped down next to his mom and began kicking his feet against the sofa.

His mother tried to ignore his annoying behavior, but it wasn't easy.

"I'm not so sure you should continue to get an allowance. You—"

Tommy leaped off the couch in total disbelief.

"You can't do that! That's my money!"

Angela remained calm as her son reacted like a human hurricane. He whirled around the room, crying and hollering. Her stern look didn't seem to faze Tommy. She quickly stood up and took him by the arm.

"Tommy, sit down, and don't say another word!"

Tommy glared at his mother. If looks could kill, even a cat with nine lives wouldn't survive this child's wrath. He began to speak but was solidly rebuked.

"Not a word!" She prayed for patience and for the right words. "I know you are doing your chores, son." A smug smile filled his face. "You are doing everything we've asked of you, for the most part." He nodded in agreement.

"Then why—" he interrupted.

"Don't," she spoke firmly. "All you think about is money. All you talk about are the things you are going to buy with it." Her tone softened as she prayed for the Lord to speak to her child. "We've told you the Lord expects part of that money to go to Him." Tommy rolled his eyes. "We haven't forced you to tithe because we believe you should give with a willing, cheerful heart."

Tommy looked as if he were about to explode. His cheeks bulged with air; it was his way of demanding to speak. His mother acquiesced.

"It's not God's money. He didn't earn it. I did! I worked real hard, and I'm going to keep it."

Angela knew it would be easier just to give Tommy his allowance. However, she also knew that this was a battle with serious spiritual consequences. If he didn't learn this lesson early in life, it would be much more difficult to learn it later.

She asked, "Where did that money come from?"

"From you guys," he responded.

"And where did we get it?"

"From Dad's job."

"And where did his company get it?"

Tommy started to answer but stopped. Then he said, "I don't understand."

Angela smiled. "That's the problem, honey. If I keep asking questions, eventually, we would have to answer, 'The money came from God.'"

Often we are just as stubborn as little Tommy. We refuse to acknowledge that what we have belongs to God, for God has said, *"The world is mine, and all that is in it"* (Ps. 50:12). We work at accumulating more and more worldly goods, often telling ourselves that if we just had a certain amount of money in the bank or various possessions that we would be content. We ignore the wisdom of the Bible on this subject. Ecclesiastes 5:10 tells us, *"Whoever loves money never has money enough; whoever loves wealth is never satisfied with his income."*

We choose to forget the destructive nature of money. Remember the consequences of greed to Ananias and Sapphira? (See Acts 5:1–10.) And who can ignore the tragedy contained in this verse: *"So Judas threw the money into the temple and left. Then he went away and hanged himself"* (Matt. 27:5)?

It's time to do some personal accounting. Which is of most value to you—knowing God and having a Spirit-filled attitude toward money or always seeking to accumulate more for your own pleasure? Are you seeking the Giver or pursuing the gifts? One good test of your spirituality is your generosity in giving to God and to His work. God promises to bless faithful stewards. Do you believe that? Really? Remember that if you truly believe it, you will act on it. Let this prayer based on Hebrews 13:5 become your own:

> Lord, please keep me free from the love of money. Help me to be content with what I have. May I never forget Your promise that You will never leave or forsake me. Having You is the greatest treasure I could ever desire. Amen.

Chapter Five

Where's the Fear?

"Fear the LORD and serve him faithfully with all your heart;
consider what great things he has done for you."
—1 Samuel 12:24

While spending forty years in the desert, Moses learned a great deal about God's ways. One day, while tending his father-in-law's flock, he saw a strange sight. A bush was on fire, but it wasn't being consumed. Curious, he moved closer for a better look. From out of the bush came God's voice—and Moses did what you or I would probably do. He hid. Moses experienced the fear of God firsthand. Later, when he led the Israelites out of Egypt, he spent considerable time teaching them about God. They, too, came to understand the fear of the Lord.

When God spoke the Ten Commandments *"from out of the fire, the cloud and the deep darkness"* (Deut. 5:22), the people trembled at the sights and sounds. They were afraid. They wanted Moses to listen to God for them and simply pass along His message. But Moses told them, *"Do not be afraid. God has come to test you, so that the fear of God will be with you to keep you from sinning"* (Exod. 20:20).

There it is in a nutshell! The fear of the Lord keeps Christians away from sin and on the straight and narrow road of holiness. Think about it for a moment. When a person truly fears God, he will not want to sin. He will

want to please God. But if he does sin, especially willful, premeditated sin, he should fear God's rebuke—unless, of course, he doesn't think God is watching that closely!

Ezekiel 8:12 describes this foolish attitude.

> *He said to me, "Son of man, have you seen what the elders of the house of Israel are doing in the darkness, each at the shrine of his own idol? They say, 'The LORD does not see us; the LORD has forsaken the land.'"*

A common attitude of a backslidden or lukewarm Christian is self-delusion. He creates a god who is different from the One revealed in Scripture. He tells himself,

- God isn't overly concerned about my every thought and action.
- It's absurd to think God can see everything, all the time.
- God is too busy in heaven to watch over my every move.
- So what if I sin a little? God is a God of love—not punishment.

Sometimes we judge the Old Testament Israelites too harshly. We can't understand their faithlessness. After all, God chose them as His people; He set them apart to proclaim His ways to an unbelieving, pagan world. Yet, today, God has set apart His church to proclaim His name to a lost and dying world. How tragic to see those in the church wallowing in darkness, saying, "God doesn't see what I do. He's not paying attention, and if He is, He forgives me anyway."

Proverbs 9:10 explains, *"The fear of the LORD is the beginning of wisdom."* Fearing the Lord is the start of a walk with Him, not something that we eventually attain when we mature in our faith. A healthy fear of God begins us on our journey toward heaven. We depend on Him to guide us onto safe spiritual ground and to keep us from straying.

To fear God means more than dreading His judgment or rebuke. It means to reverence Him, to be in awe of

Him, to worship Him. Our fear of God changes as we come to know Him more intimately. At first, we are afraid of Him. Just like Moses at the burning bush, we want to hide from the presence of God. But when we come to Him in repentance and receive His gift of salvation, our fear turns to awe. We worship the One who loves us so much that He gave His life to redeem us from sin. As we walk in close fellowship with Him, we have a respect for His commands; it becomes our souls' desire to please and honor Him. Our fear of God increases because we come to realize who God is. At the same time, we no longer dread His punishment because we have a Father-child relationship with Him. We marvel at all He has done for us, and we trust Him to keep us in His care.

Without a godly dread, though, we would not come to know Him as our Father. A proper fear can lead us to a relationship with God. A lack of fear can keep us from ever knowing Him.

"I'm tired of their stupid rules!" vented David, his eyes captivated by the race car on the video game. As his fingers expertly maneuvered the car around the racetrack on the screen, he grumbled, "When I'm a parent, I'm going to let my kids make their own decisions."

Abby, his neighbor and best friend, sat motionless on the living room chair. She wanted to help and figured listening was a good place to start.

David glanced at her for a second, causing his car to crash into a brick wall. He cursed under his breath as he flung the video game controller onto the floor.

"That's the fifth time in a row I've hit that wall."

Abby took a deep breath. She stared at David with a mixture of compassion and frustration.

"Reminds me of your life right now."

David was silent. Only Abby could get away with that kind of talk...the truth. Although she wasn't his girlfriend, he hoped that would change before long.

"Why are you on my case?" David got up and began pacing around the room. "It's bad enough that I have to listen to my parents. Don't you start preaching to me, too."

Abby shook her head. David read her reaction loud and clear. It said, "Warning! Lecture coming! Take cover immediately!" He turned away, reaching to retrieve the joystick to resume his game.

"Oh, that's real mature, David. Shut me out, just like you're trying to shut out God. I imagine He's getting tired of your attitude, too." David focused on the screen, trying to ignore Abby's comments. "I've noticed a real change in you over the last several months." She hesitated, searching for the right words. "I'm worried about you, David. I feel like I don't know you anymore."

Her words unnerved David. He bit his lip as his mind raced with anxiety. Was she going to break off their friendship? He swallowed hard.

"I'm sorry, Abby. It just seems like everything is going wrong. I'm not happy anymore, and I don't know what to do."

"David, listen to me. You're not happy because you're not obeying your parents or God. You don't seem to respect anybody, except maybe me."

He turned abruptly away from the TV. "Maybe I don't like anybody else. Maybe I'm just fed up with being told what to do."

Abby had been praying for an opportunity to talk to David. It seemed as if the Holy Spirit was opening the door for her right now.

"David, if you really trust me, then hear me out." He didn't look too responsive, but she wasn't discouraged. "I think a big problem of yours is that you don't have a fear of God. Lately, you've been living your life like there's no tomorrow." His face turned pale. "Do you really think you're going to make it to heaven when you treat God with such disrespect?"

David protested, "I gave my heart to the Lord when I was ten years old! I went to the altar. What more do I have to do?"

"Maybe you did go forward, David, but did you ever think that your conversion experience was nothing more than blind emotionalism? Why did you go to the altar in the first place?"

Before he could think, David blurted out, "Because all my friends went! And I knew it would make my parents happy."

David collapsed against the sofa. He couldn't believe what he'd just said.

"So...you're not saved...and you know it," Abby said gently, not wanting to quench the Spirit.

David slowly nodded. "I guess not." Several seconds of silence turned into minutes. Abby wanted to say something, but the Holy Spirit said, "Wait." God was working in David, and she didn't want to get in the way.

"How did you know I wasn't a Christian?" David questioned, startling Abby with his directness.

"Because you don't act like one," she answered softly.

"How am I supposed to act?" he asked.

"Kind, gentle, loving, giving—you know, like Jesus."

"Oh," mumbled David.

"Do you fear God?"

"What do you mean?"

Abby knew David wasn't dumb. He had gone to church for years, yet it seemed that the simple truths of God alluded him.

"Well, are you looking forward to meeting Him on Judgment Day?"

David looked puzzled.

"Not really. I mean, I'm not looking forward to dying, if that's what you mean."

Without batting an eye, Abby said, "People who love Jesus—you know, real Christians—they look forward to seeing Him. Think about it, David. When we get to heaven, we will see Jesus face-to-face. Who wouldn't be excited about that?"

"Then where does this fear stuff come in? If you love God so much, why would you be afraid of Him?"

Abby's response was wiser than her years. "Most people are afraid when they encounter God. Adam and Eve were, along with most of the prophets." Her gentle tone soothed David. "Sin makes us feel guilty. It's like when you were a child and your parents caught you doing something wrong. You were scared because you knew you were going to get it."

David chuckled, "I'm still scared of Dad. I can't figure out how he catches me at stuff."

Abby smiled and took a deep breath. "Then you know what it's like to be punished...and you don't want to go through that again. That fear kept you from doing the same stupid thing again. That's part of what it means to fear God."

David nodded his understanding.

"David, when you die—and you will one day—you will meet Jesus Christ. If you haven't really given your life to Him, then you will go to hell. If you would only think about it, then you would start seeing the truth. Then you would start fearing God and hell—and you would ask God to save you right now so you don't go there."

David stared into Abby's deep blue eyes. She wasn't sure what he was thinking, but she continued.

"Do you want to go to heaven?"

He shrugged his shoulders and replied, "I don't know."

"Do you care if you go to heaven?"

"Sometimes," he said quietly.

"So tell me, what *do* you care about?"

"That's easy. Video games, football, and..." His eyes began to glow. "And you." A shy smile appeared on his face as he watched for her reaction. "Can we forget about this God stuff right now? I'm not in the mood to talk about it."

Abby knew that David wasn't ready to make a commitment to the Lord. She prayed that he would not wait until it was too late. Getting up from her chair, she walked slowly toward the door.

"I think I'd better be going now. Please think about what we've talked about, David." Her eyes teared over. "One day, you are going to wish that you had taken God seriously. Don't wait until it's too late."

"You're awfully cute when you're serious," he called as the door was closing.

David turned back to his video game.

Like millions of others who are lost, he was too focused on this life to think about his eternal soul. Consequently, he didn't fear God's judgment. He didn't see God for who He really is. David was like many people who create their own visions of God in order to appease their sinful natures. Instead of respecting God and serving Him, they think of God as—

- the man upstairs,
- the big guy in heaven,
- an impersonal spirit, or
- a benevolent grandfather with a long, white beard.

One cannot have a fear of God without understanding His nature, His requirements, and His hatred for sin and rebellion. Please notice I said, "hatred for sin," not "hatred for sinners." Since many people make up their own versions of God, fear is not an emotion they associate with their Creator. But the Bible teaches that every individual must consider the implications of his sinful actions, his eternal destination after death, and God's promised face-to-face meeting that is coming for every person one day. Romans 14:11–12 tells us,

> "'As surely as I live,' says the Lord, 'every knee will bow before me; every tongue will confess to God.'" So then, each of us will give an account of himself to God.

Every human being will stand before God and be held accountable for his actions. It doesn't matter if he is the president of the United States, a CEO of a major international corporation, or a Hollywood movie star; everyone will stand before the Judge. God's Word says, *"God does not show favoritism"* (Acts 10:34). How many can say they are ready to meet their Maker? Jesus Christ warned His disciples and the multitudes surrounding Him to carefully consider their lifestyles. He said,

> *There is nothing concealed that will not be disclosed, or hidden that will not be made known. What you have said in the dark will be heard in the daylight, and what you have whispered in the ear in the inner rooms will be proclaimed from the roofs. I tell you, my friends, do not be afraid of those who kill the body and after that can do no more. But I will show you whom you should fear: Fear him who, after the killing of the body, has power to throw you into hell. Yes, I tell you, fear him.*
> (Luke 12:2–5)

Some describe the fear of God in only one way; that is, as an awe and respect for Him. Although that is certainly true and biblical, many lost in church today completely discount the "other side" of God. Hell is real, and only God has the power to send people there. Satan has been working overtime, mocking those who preach or believe in a literal hell. Yet without the threat of hell, the fear of God is quite useless. Why fear God if there's no eternal punishment or damnation? Why fear God if He doesn't control your final destiny? Again, a distorted view of God promoted by the evil one prevents people from understanding this truth.

In my years in the ministry, I've found many people who want to hear the truth no matter "how bad it hurts." But all too often, many lost in mega-church cathedrals as well as small country chapels would rather hear messages that tickle their ears. As this world spirals closer to the Age of the Antichrist, the Bible clearly predicts a great apostasy before the revealing of the dark one. I believe we are living in these times. Thus Paul's warning to Timothy is relevant to us today.

> *For the time will come when men will not put up with sound doctrine. Instead, to suit their own desires, they will gather around them a great number of teachers to say what their itching ears want to hear. They will turn their ears away from the truth and turn aside to myths.*
> (2 Tim. 4:3–4)

Let's look at some of the key phrases from this passage. First, consider the term *"sound doctrine."* One of the basic foundations of the Old Testament is the fear of God. Jesus Christ did not change this principle; in fact, He upheld it. Sound doctrine can be achieved only through a careful, prayerful study of the Word of God. If you find that your beliefs contradict the Bible, then you are mistaken and have misinterpreted Scripture. Sound doctrine is not revealed through our circumstances, our emotions or feelings, or our lives; but only through the Bible. Satan must salivate at the lost in church—those who don't understand the power behind the Word of God. Do you understand why you believe what you believe? Do you even know what you believe? Study the Bible, and the *"sound doctrine"* of the fear of God will grow in you like a well-watered seed planted in fertile ground.

Another term Paul used was *"own desires."* Human beings are naturally rebellious creatures. Anybody who has parented a two-year-old child knows what I mean. Our flesh-oriented desires seldom if ever line up with God's will. As Jeremiah 17:9 states, *"The heart is deceitful above all things, and desperately wicked; who can know it?"* (NKJV). The lost in church allow their desires to saddle them into sin, making them unable and unwilling to come to the cross of Calvary. Jesus called people to deny themselves. We can please God only when we fear

Him and allow His transforming power to take over our desires.

Paul also wrote about *"itching ears."* Isn't it wonderful when people tell you what you want to hear? "Oh, that blouse is so beautiful," or "You look very handsome in that suit." At our jobs, we love to hear comments like, "You are the best at what you do; keep it up!" Whether it's about our appearance, our jobs, homes, children, pets, or anything else we consider to be valuable, we love to be complimented and recognized. What about God's Word? Do we want to hear His truth about obedience and judgment or talk only about His love and mercy? The lost in church have this attitude: "Tell me what I want to hear—something that doesn't make me feel guilty or something that will allow me to keep my current lifestyle." In other words, "Don't give me the truth. Tell me comfortable little lies." The last thing the lost in church want is to be yanked out of their comfort zones by the Truth. When they encounter it, they use Satan's deceitful response, "Well, that's your interpretation!"

Paul wrote that men will *"gather around them a great number of teachers."* Since many people lost in church don't want to hear the truth of God's expectations of His children, they turn to those who will tell them what they *want* to hear instead of what they *need* to hear. These lost souls will intentionally surround themselves with people who make them feel good under the theological banners of love, tolerance, and peace. They think that it's more important to get along with as many people as possible than to get the facts right about God's standards. This is all backward, which, of course, is what Satan wants. Our first priority is to find God. Then God will help us to get along better with others. Remember, it is your responsibility to understand God's ways and to choose wisely whom you accept as a pastor and teacher. Seek God on this matter. He will not let you down. The last thing the Lord wants in your life is false prophets, wolves in sheep's clothing, whose only purpose is to deceive and destroy. False prophets do not teach a proper fear of God.

Paul said that these false teachers would turn people toward *"myths."* A myth, or fable, is an imaginative story completely made up by man. It's often based on truth, but over the years the truth has been watered down and distorted into a form far different from its origin. Those who love the Lord and His Word can see this infectious, poisonous trend sweeping across the globe like an unstoppable spiritual plague. The fear of God is being replaced with emotional appeals from the pulpit, Hollywood-style productions yielding little spiritual fruit, and cultural relativism, which calls absolute truths old-fashioned and outdated.

My dog Stormy shows more of a healthy fear of her master than many in the church do toward God. Here's a recent example.

"Honey, would you go downstairs and get the laundry?" asked Tina, my wife.

"Sure," I responded, getting up from my chair and heading toward the steps.

When I reached the top of the stairs, I noticed Stormy at the bottom, staring sheepishly in my direction.

I said, "Hey, Stormy, you being a good dog?"

As I walked down the steps, Stormy froze, one paw still resting on the first step. Her medium-sized frame trembled as I passed her at the bottom of the staircase.

"Stormy, what did you do?" I questioned as I watched her tail curl under her stomach.

She recognized the tone in my voice and took off for safety, under our bed! I instantly took a detour from the laundry room and went into the kitchen. I knew my dog well. Her favorite hobby—one she knows is against the rules—is raiding the kitchen trash can. With food of varying colors, she had used the kitchen floor like a painter uses his palette. Oh yes, she was an artist, a con artist!

Isn't it interesting? My dog, a mere animal without a soul in need of salvation, without the ability to critically think as a human, without any prodding from the Holy Spirit, knows to fear her master! Sadly, the lost in church don't fear their Master. If they did, many would not do the things they do. Read how the Bible describes this condition:

> *The Spirit clearly says that in later times some will abandon the faith and follow deceiving spirits and things taught by demons. Such teachings come through hypocritical liars, whose consciences have been seared as with a hot iron.* (1 Tim. 4:1–2)

When the human conscience has been scorched and scarred by sin, it is almost impossible for it to respond with any fear of God. Jeremiah 8:7 reads,

> *Even the stork in the heavens knows her appointed times; and the turtledove, the swift, and the swallow observe the time of their coming. But My people do not know the judgment of the LORD.* (NKJV)

Ouch! Remember, these are the words of God Almighty. Those who don't have a fear of God certainly do not believe in *"the judgment of the LORD."* Punishment and discipline are not pleasant, but they will call us back to the straight and narrow road; that is, if our attitudes are right. This harsh observation from God must be taken seriously! The animals have more wisdom and insight than those who claim to know God but don't. Read Jeremiah's next words carefully:

> *How can you say, "We are wise, and the law of the LORD is with us"? Look, the false pen of the scribe certainly works falsehood. The wise men are ashamed, they are dismayed and taken. Behold, they have rejected the word of the LORD; so what wisdom do they have?* (Jer. 8:8–9 NKVJ)

Jeremiah's words were for the Israelites. Although they were God's chosen people, they were not serving Him. They came through the doors of His temple in order to worship idols. They had a form of religion, but it was powerless to change their lives and lead them in righteous ways. As relevant as these words were to the people of Jeremiah's day, they strike at the heart of the lost in church today. Let us allow Jeremiah's words to shine God's light into our minds and hearts.

Jeremiah asked the people how they could say they were wise. Yet they honestly believed they were. They presumed to possess wisdom from above. Scripture, though, reveals that without the fear of the Lord, there is no wisdom. They claimed God's law as their beacon of light; sadly, they didn't know or understand His law. How many today assume that because they attend church that they know the Bible? Do they spend time studying it, or does it sit on their bookshelves collecting dust?

The people in Jeremiah's day chose to believe lies, transcribed by the *"false pen"* of scribes. These scribes were the guardians of God's precious words. They didn't have copy machines, huge printing presses, or any of the other modern conveniences of the printing trade. They didn't even have ballpoint pens or No. 2 pencils. So these highly religious men would copy the scrolls of the Old Testament sentence for sentence, word for word, syllable for syllable. During the times of apostasy and national rebellion, many of Israel's kings would order these transcribers to "rewrite" or "reword" or "slightly change" the words and thus their meanings. Others would simply take the scrolls out of public circulation, leaving the Israelites without divine guidance. Satan is still working overtime today trying to distort the words of our Lord. Thus many lost in the church today don't understand the fear of the Lord; they don't know that it *"is the beginning of wisdom"* (Ps. 111:10; Prov. 9:10).

As I was reading a Christian book by a well-meaning, well-liked Christian author, a statement he made amazed me. In paraphrased form, it said something like this: "We don't need to fear God because He has taken our sins and nailed them to the cross." I understand the point the author was trying to make, but I would add that *because* God has taken our sins and nailed them to the cross, we should fear—revere and stand in awe of—Him.

The fear of God, as well as our love for Him, leads us toward holiness. Fearing punishment and the consequences of sin is wise and prudent, as one of the thieves at Calvary understood. In Luke 23:39–43, we find a record of the story.

> *One of the criminals who hung there hurled insults at him: "Aren't you the Christ? Save yourself and us!" But the other criminal rebuked him. "Don't you **fear God**," he said, "since you are under the same sentence? We are punished justly, for we are getting what our deeds deserve. But this man has done nothing wrong." Then he said, "Jesus, remember me when you come into your kingdom." Jesus answered him, "I tell you the truth, today you will be with me in paradise."*
>
> (emphasis added)

When a person rejects God's inspired Word, he can make up whatever religious system he desires. The outcome of this spiritual travesty is a lost soul. The lost in church exhibit the same characteristics as the scribes who rejected the Scriptures. They, too, are ashamed, dismayed, and taken.

First, they are *"ashamed."* They hide from God because of their sin and unwillingness to repent. You don't see this emotion outwardly. The feeling is deep inside the heart, and it creates tremendous anxiety.

Second, they are *"dismayed."* Their guilt and lack of joy begins to eat away at their false peace. Depression is often the result.

Finally, they are *"taken"* (*"trapped,"* NIV). Once this type of thinking occurs, it becomes lodged in a person's mind like a Rocky Mountain tick on a dog. It grabs its victim, sinks its teeth into him, and will not let go until something much bigger than itself frees him of its influence.

There is a direct link between having a fear of the Lord and studying the Bible. There is no easy way to grow in the fear and the knowledge of the Lord. It comes through years of faithful study and service; obedience, even when it's difficult to obey; and a humble attitude that is willing to accept correction. Without the fear of the Lord, people cannot fully grasp God's ways, His holiness, His discipline, or His expectations. A life without this fear is a compromised life of ambiguity. Christianity must include a healthy dose of godly fear to produce the heavenly fruit God expects from each of His followers. Without the fear of God deeply ingrained in our hearts, our view of God is tainted. Instead of confidently walking the straight and narrow path that leads to heaven, we will weave, hobble, and stumble along.

Amber and Sicily were the talk of a small Midwestern town. Since their birth, the twins had captured attention wherever they went. Their angelic smiles could melt the coldest heart.

Their parents, Bryan and Susie, were extra proud of their "pumpkins," as they liked to call them. They enjoyed all the attention that their toddlers received.

Because the twins were identical in appearance, most people hadn't noticed the differences in their personalities. Amber was quiet, content, and obedient; but Sicily was noisy, rambunctious, and defiant.

One Saturday, Bryan was outside washing the family car while the girls played nearby. Every few minutes, like clockwork, Susie would glance out the front window to check on the girls. She knew Bryan occasionally got too engrossed in his chores to watch the twins carefully. She opened the front door and reminded him, "Watch the girls, please."

Bryan waved at her as he continued to wash the car. He glanced at the twins for a moment. "They're fine, honey."

Susie watched a car whiz by. "Those teenagers are crazy, Bryan. Don't take your eyes off the kids, especially Sicily."

Bryan nodded again. "Gotcha, honey."

Sicily and Amber were sitting on the ground, their dolls surrounding them. Across the street, a German Shepherd caught Sicily's eye. She had seen dogs before, but none this large and beautiful.

Sicily smiled at Amber. "See doggy. Pretty. Go see."

Amber glanced at the dog before her gaze returned to Sicily. "No go, Sicily. Daddy says not cross street." She frowned. "Bad...bad."

Sicily's eyes were fixed on the dog. He was so cute. She jumped up.

"Doggy," she giggled, toddling toward the dog—and the street.

Amber cried, "No, Sissy, no!"

Bryan jerked his head toward the commotion. He screamed, "Sicily, stop!"

Sicily's legs were running full throttle. She heard her father, yet the dog's appeal won out.

"Stop, baby, stop!" he shouted.

"Doggy...doggy," she cooed.

Bryan sprinted toward her, his heart racing with fear. Suddenly, a fast-moving sports car appeared around the curve—only a hundred yards or so from their house.

Amber's piercing cry caused Sicily to stop at the edge of the road. She turned for a moment, confused by her sister's wailing. Then, ignoring her father's voice and her sister's cries, she stepped into the street. Suddenly, Bryan scooped her into his arms as the car whizzed by them. The sound of screeching tires scared Sicily, and she began to cry. She pointed toward the car, then toward the dog.

"Doggy, Daddy...doggy, Daddy."

Bryan held her tightly as tears streamed down his face. "How many times have I told you not to go near the street?"

Through her tears, Sicily sobbed, "Doggy, Daddy. I want doggy."

It's easy to see which child had a proper fear of authority—a fear that kept her safe, even from dangers she didn't fully comprehend. The fear of God keeps us on the path of peace, joy, and safety—safety from sin, from the devil, and from ourselves. Just as Eve surveyed the desirous and appetizing fruit, little Sicily gazed on the German Shepherd without considering the consequences of her actions. The fear of God keeps our eyes on Jesus and away from the enticing things of the world. Often, we may not understand why God says no to certain things, but we can rest assured that He knows what is best for us. Because Sicily was just a child, her knowledge of danger and evil was minimal. The church has no such excuse.

God desires a special relationship with you, one based on love, trust, obedience, and holy reverence. When you obey your Father's commands, you have no need to fear His punishment. As 1 John 4:16–18 says,

> *Whoever lives in love lives in God, and God in him. In this way, love is made complete among us so that we will have confidence on the day of judgment, because in this world we are like him. There is no fear in love. But perfect love drives out fear, because fear has to do with punishment. The one who fears is not made perfect in love.*

So we are left with this paradox: We are charged to *"fear God and keep his commandments"* (Eccl. 12:13) while having a love for Him that takes away our fear.

Isn't that just like God? As you give Him your fear, He will bless you with His love.

The lost in church need to consider the day they will leave this life. Do they fear it or look forward to it? God wants the church to come in childlike faith toward Him; His arms are open and waiting. Are you running to Him or from Him?

Chapter Six

Grace or Gossip?

"A word aptly spoken is like apples of gold
in settings of silver."
—Proverbs 25:11

A soft breeze drifted through the outdoor café, located in an upscale Chicago suburb. Four ladies dressed in their finest were finishing a late lunch, leisurely sipping their coffee. Devoted mothers and wives, all four were long-standing members of Grace Church in Oak Park. For several years now, they had been meeting for a mid-week lunch to encourage one another, and, perhaps more important, to share the latest "news."

Samantha Beddington was the unofficial leader of the group. Although the oldest, she was undoubtedly the most beautiful—and the one with the best connections socially. Her elegantly coiffured dark hair caught the afternoon light as she turned to speak.

"So what's the latest with your neighbors, Sally?"

Sally's usual smile dimmed a bit. "Oh, you girls just won't believe it." She shook her head sadly as she looked around the table.

Samantha placed her finger on the edge of her coffee cup and slowly caressed the outside rim. Her nervous habit betrayed her calm exterior as she anticipated some "juicy" news. The other ladies, Vicki and Barb, eagerly gave Sally their full attention.

Sally began, "Well, from what I hear, Brad and Cindy are seeing a marriage counselor."

Vicki spoke up immediately, "What's the trouble?"

"I'm not sure, but the rumors are flying on my street." Sally paused, relishing the limelight and wanting to extend the moment.

"Well?" asked Samantha with a hint of impatience.

The ladies unconsciously leaned toward Sally as she continued.

"I'm not one to spread rumors, so I'll ask you to keep this to yourselves." She waited for their mutual consent. "I'm sure you'll all want to pray about this. As you know, Cindy and Brad have been respected members of Grace Church for over five years, but now some are saying that Brad has eyes for the pastor's wife."

In unison, their mouths dropped in astonishment. They reacted to the news like famished lionesses being tossed a succulent filet mignon.

Samantha gasped, "Where did you hear that?"

Sally glanced at the tables near them to make sure their conversation remained private.

"Girls, I can't tell you everything right now." She ignored the voice of her conscience as she proceeded to drop strong hints. "Just suffice it to say that this is big news, and I know from reliable sources that it's true." Her face flushed as she added, "I've even heard the affair has already begun!"

Barb couldn't hold back her tongue. "Do you think Pastor Simms knows?"

Samantha sat back in her chair. She tried to conceal her excitement; after all, this was a scandal in the making. In her mind, these lunch-hour socials served as prayer meetings, designed to gather and distribute information for spiritual purposes. This was church work—more than that, it was God's work!

"How many people know about this?" Samantha asked, as a look of dread covered her face.

Vicki shook her head as she spoke up. "Maybe I shouldn't be saying this, but I feel I must." In a conspiratorial tone, she whispered, "One of my friends in the choir told me someone told her that Brad and the pastor's wife were seen together...at a hotel in Rockford."

They stared at each other in "holy" disbelief. For a few minutes, no one spoke.

Then Samantha took charge. "This is terrible, just terrible. I was afraid something like this was going on. Haven't you all noticed the pastor's messages going downhill lately? I think he knows the truth and doesn't know what to do." She glanced around the table. "Don't tell anybody any of this except your closest friends—people you trust— those who you know will pray earnestly about this."

Just as Samantha was finishing her sentence, she noticed Barb's face turn pale. When she turned to see what had startled Barb, Samantha saw Pastor Simms approaching their table.

"Well, ladies, it's so nice to see you. It looks like you are deep in conversation." His tone was pleasant, but he seemed more reserved than usual.

Samantha nearly choked. The other ladies smiled nervously as the pastor stood over them. They wondered if he knew what they had been talking about.

Struggling for the right words, Samantha said, "Oh, Pastor Simms, surely you wouldn't want to know about our girl talk."

Sensing her discomfort, the pastor asked gently, "Is it anything I can help you with?"

The other ladies were struck with fear as Samantha tried to diffuse the tension.

"No, no," Samantha stumbled. Her normal levelheadedness was beginning to falter. "It's personal business." She glanced at the others. "It should probably be kept among us. We don't want be gossiping, you know."

Pastor Simms hesitated, then said, "Well, all right. I'll see you all in church on Sunday. Enjoy your afternoon."

As he began to walk away, Samantha said, "We'll look forward to it. By the way, what are you going to preach on this week?"

He stopped, and for a moment he didn't move. As the pastor slowly began to turn back toward them, it was obvious that he was carefully weighing his words.

"It will be a surprise. You ladies have just given me a wonderful idea that's long overdue for a sermon."

Although Pastor Simms had not heard the details of their conversation, he surmised from their obvious discomfort that they had been gossiping. What made his concern even greater was his fear that as Christians they had come to regard an evil practice as acceptable.

Many in the church today have difficulty recognizing gossip for what it is. In our age of advanced and lightning-fast communication, humankind still resorts to the age-old habit of gossip—in spite of the Bible's warnings: *"Like a club or a sword or a sharp arrow is the man who gives false testimony against his neighbor"* (Prov. 25:18). *"A gossip separates close friends"* (Prov. 16:28). *"Whoever spreads slander is a fool"* (Prov. 10:18).

Most gossip starts off innocently enough. It begins with a friendly conversation, but then it deteriorates into innuendoes and false allegations. Gossip not only harms others but also damages those who participate in it. Although gossip can have devastating results, many people make excuses for their behavior, such as...

- I need to tell others so they can pray about the situation.
- I didn't mean to be unkind; I was just trying to help.
- It's the truth, isn't it?
- I was only talking. You're way too legalistic.
- I didn't start it; I'm just repeating what I heard.
- I'm just seeking advice so I know how I can help them.

Consider how *"false testimony"* and malicious actions often go together in their damaging effects on a person's life.

Dean was captain of the football team, in the top ten of his graduating class, and on his way to Penn State with a full scholarship. He was the all-American boy with a bright future. Popular with the girls, well liked by his teachers, and respected by his neighbors, he never had reason to doubt his success or the loyalty of his friends.

"Hey, Dean, we need to talk," called a voice from down the hallway.

Dean turned and smiled. "Sure, what's up, Keith?"

His friend and teammate pointed to an empty classroom and suggested they go there to talk. The look on Keith's face made Dean uneasy.

"Somebody told me something you've got to hear." The concern in Keith's eyes spoke louder than his words.

Before Dean could reply, his mind spiraled into a series of "what-ifs." Was his girlfriend cheating on him? Did he flunk a test? Was the coach mad at him?

"What's going on, man?" asked Dean. "You're making me nervous."

Keith didn't want to be the one to break it to him, but he had little choice. After all, they were friends, and Dean needed to know the truth. He gently placed his hand on Dean's shoulder and looked him in the eyes.

"There's talk around school that you're into drugs."

"What? You've got to be kidding! People have to know that's not true. Some dopehead probably started the rumor as a stupid joke."

Keith's reaction was not what Dean had expected. He tightened his grip on Dean's shoulder.

"Dean, that's not all of it. There are pictures circulating of you in your car—holding a joint." Dean couldn't believe what he was hearing. "The principal has them."

Dean sagged against the wall. The color left his face as he began to understand the implications of Keith's words.

"But, Keith, you know it's not true. I'd never—"

"I know, Dean, but that's not the point. I'm thinking of your scholarship—and your Christian witness. It doesn't matter if it's true or not. A lot of people out there are jealous as all get-out of you. They love this stuff, man. It makes them feel…" He shook his head, searching for the right words. "It makes them feel good to see you go down. Don't you get it? It's a power thing."

Dean closed his eyes and took a long, deep breath. He realized how devastating this lie could be to his Christian witness, his girl, his college scholarship, his friends and family—they would all suffer.

A lump formed in Dean's throat. "How many of our friends are buying it?"

Keith wished he didn't have to answer. This was the hardest thing he had ever had to do. Dean looked like a five-year-old boy who had just witnessed his dog being run over by a car.

"More than you want to know. I'm sorry, buddy. I'll do what I can, but you know how it is once a rumor gets started. I've got to get going now. Take it easy."

Dean resembled a statue as he watched his best friend turn away. He was cold, numb, and scared. Suddenly, a voice interrupted his shock.

"Dean, I need to see you in my office, pronto!" barked the principal in an unfamiliar, authoritative tone.

Dean jerked his head around and met the principal's cold eyes head-on.

"Yes, sir," he replied.

As they walked down the hall toward the office, students stopped what they were doing and stared at him. Some whispered, some smugly smiled, while others turned away in disgust. His whole world was coming apart in front of him. As they neared the office door, he spotted his girlfriend, Reba. She would be his one shelter, his one real friend. He could count on her. Then he saw the disappointment in her eyes.

"Dean, how could you do this?" she sobbed.

The principal shook his head and stared at Dean.

"You've got a lot of explaining to do, young man."

For the first time, Dean felt as if his world were crumbling. His joy was stolen, his peace was shattered, and his future was now in question. One lie uttered in the dark; one doctored, fraudulent photograph; one individual with ugly motives and intense jealousy; and willing, itching ears coveting the "inside scoop" had all come together. Now, one life—his—was damaged, perhaps beyond repair.

Dean was in a daze as the principal escorted him into his office, closed the door firmly, and sat down behind his desk.

"Please have a seat, Mr. Ridge."

Principal Kline had never called him that before. He had always used his first name—until now. Dean's tongue seemed to swell, and his erratic breathing made it hard to talk.

He managed to whisper, "Thank you, sir."

The principal opened the bottom drawer of his desk and pulled something from it. Dean watched as he tossed it toward him.

"Would you care to explain this?"

Dean clutched the photograph and tried to focus. Sure enough, there he was in his car on the school parking lot, with a marijuana joint in his mouth. He brought the picture closer and squinted, trying to see some flaw in it. He knew the picture of him was real, but the joint must have been superimposed into the photo.

"Obviously, it's...a...sick joke," he stammered, wanting to tear it up into a million pieces.

"I see," said the principal, unimpressed with Dean's feeble explanation.

Dean jumped up. "Oh, come on, of course that's me, but somebody placed that..." his voice began to carry into the hallway, "that drug into the photo. It's easy to do with the right equipment."

The painful expression on the principal's face didn't subside. He reached into his desk again and pulled out a bag of marijuana.

"How do you explain this?"

"What's that?" questioned Dean, genuine confusion filling his face.

The principal's patience rapidly deteriorated. The disappointment in his voice was obvious as he added, "We found it in your locker a couple of hours ago."

Dean's confusion quickly gave way to raw anger. He wanted justice. He wanted the truth. He refused to believe this was happening to him—and his friends were buying it hook, line, and sinker. Dozens of his friends knew the combination to his locker. He knew he was innocent, and God knew he was innocent, but how could he convince everyone else? Even if this whole mess was straightened out, Dean knew he would never be the same.

What a tragedy! This kind of devastation is repeated in one way or another countless times a day. It takes just one individual to ruin another person's reputation. Imagine how news of this sort would have spread across that school. Juicy gossip, although a lie from hell, can quickly capture people in its web of deceit. Lies or half-truths destroy innocent victims, leaving rage, bitterness, and unforgiveness in their nasty wakes.

Consider what would have happened if the individuals who first heard the lie simply would have refused to believe it or to pass on the rumor. They could have kept it to themselves, or better yet, prayed for God's direction and talked to Dean directly. These actions might have prevented the situation from getting out of control. Like a small spark among a dry forest, gossip spreads rapidly and can quickly turn into a raging inferno. As James 3:5 says, *"The tongue is a little member and boasts great things. See how great a forest a little fire kindles!"* (NKJV).

To see how gossip can be prevented, we first need to understand why people gossip. One reason is that *they want the inside scoop.* Have you noticed how some people always seem to know what's going on in other people's lives? They invest a great deal of time in order to "be in the know." Although some of these individuals are motivated by real concern and the desire to help, others crave the sense of importance they feel from being one of the first to hear the latest news. Perhaps this explains the growing television audiences for entertainment-style programs (essentially gossip-filled shows) and the shrinking audiences for factual news shows.

Spreading gossip makes some people feel important. Knowing the latest news about other people allows them to feel part of their community. It helps them to feel connected to a group and provides a false sense of self-worth. The next time someone is anxious to tell you a piece of mouth-watering information, watch his or her face closely. The adrenaline rush caused by spreading gossip is a sight to behold.

Gossiping gives them power. A basic sinful human instinct is to crave power. Without the Holy Spirit's influence in our lives, we naturally revert to such base desires. Spreading gossip gives an individual power over the willing listener as well as over the person about whom he is talking. The gossip has something the listener wants, something some people even lust over. In addition, the gossip holds another person's reputation—possibly even that person's future—in his hands.

Gossip makes boring lives seem more exciting. There is no doubt that most gossip, although untrue, is exciting, exhilarating, and simply too good to pass up. This is why soap operas are so popular. Vicariously, people derive excitement from them. They are intrigued by such questions as, Who is sleeping with whom? Who is the father of the baby? What lie will be uncovered today? And the list of tantalizing topics goes on.

Sharing gossip that is based on truth makes some people feel more spiritual. The lost in church often spread ugly truths about other church members under the guise of compassion and caring. This is one of Satan's most seductive tools. Gossips feel closer to God by sending "prayer requests" to their friends and neighbors describing the nasty details of another person's problems. What is purely an emotional response, or a sinful "high," masquerades as love and concern. Consider the warning the Bible gives to young widows that also can have application to our lives:

> They have begun to grow wanton against Christ,... having condemnation because they have cast off their first faith. And besides they learn to be idle, wandering about from house to house, and not only idle but also gossips and busybodies, saying things which they ought not....For some have already turned aside after Satan. (1 Tim. 5:11–13, 15 NKJV)

Well-meaning people from every walk of life, denomination, and age group gossip for "all the right reasons." Although their purpose may be noble in their eyes, the fruit of their actions is evil. Some of you may say, "Hey, wait a minute. You're really being judgmental." The Word of God doesn't water down the truth. Read the passage from 1 Timothy again. God sees our attitudes, motives, and actions in an entirely different light than we often do. Let's take a closer look at these verses.

"Condemnation"—God condemns gossips. Their actions are not motivated by the Holy Spirit or by faith. Romans 14:23 reminds us that *"whatever is not from faith is sin"* (NKJV). People who gossip damage other people's reputations. This action is not motivated by love, but by hatred. First John 4:20 states, *"If someone says, 'I love God,' and hates his brother, he is a liar; for he who does not love his brother whom he has seen, how can he love God whom he has not seen?"*

"Cast off their first faith"—Here's a picture of seeds that have been planted among thorns, cast on the rocks, or scorched by the heat of the sun. There may be an

appearance of faith, but the works are not from God. A gossip not only spits into the face of the one whom he is gossiping about but also spits on the Son of Man. (Of course, I'm speaking in spiritual terms.) Imagine you're walking along the road, and you spot something shiny in the grass. You quickly run over and pick up what you hope is a valuable coin, but it turns out to be a useless piece of metal. You toss it back on the curb, or cast it aside. In the same way, gossips toss aside the grace of God as worthless.

"Idle" and *"wandering"*—A Christian who is right with God has a purpose in life, and that is to follow the Lord wherever He leads. The Holy Spirit will guide you; He will prevent you from losing your course like a ship lost in a storm. Gossips have too much time on their hands, and they use that extra time to fulfill the lusts of the flesh. Most don't have a purpose in life because their fellowship with the Lord is minimal or non-existent. God expects us to fill our time with activities that bring Him glory and not shame. If you don't have a clear direction from the Lord, seek Him with your entire heart, mind, and soul. Remember, idleness breeds sin. *"Do not give the devil a foothold"* (Eph. 4:27).

"Turned aside after Satan"—The devil, who is called a *"roaring lion"* in 1 Peter 5:8, often comes as an *"angel of light"* (2 Cor. 11:14), calling well-meaning men and women to do his bidding. The Bible clearly states that busybodies and gossips turn their allegiance over to Satan by spreading lies, rumors, half-truths, or unkind and hurtful truths. Since his fall, Satan's strategies haven't changed. His plan has always been to deceive the apple of God's eye, which is humankind, and turn people against one another and against their Creator. It may appear harsh at first glance, but this verse clearly states that gossips are turning to Satan. This is not something one would want on his spiritual résumé as he tries to enter heaven. Sadly, this practice keeps people out of

heaven altogether. Gossips aren't loving their neighbors; they're loathing them.

You may be asking yourself, "How in the world do I know when I'm gossiping? Is there some rule of thumb?" The answer is an unequivocal yes!

You are gossiping when you are speaking about someone's problems without having his unconditional approval to do so.

You are gossiping when you tell others to pray for somebody when that person didn't ask you to spread the word about his situation.

You are gossiping when you tell your best friend a confidential piece of information about somebody else.

You are contributing to gossip when you ask another individual about somebody else's personal business that you have no right to know.

You are participating in gossip when you open your ears to somebody else's gossip.

You are a party to gossip when you hear others speaking unkindly about another person and yet keep silent. Think about the times when you could have come to someone's defense or stopped gossip in its tracks. Gossip is much more prevalent than most of us realize, but we have become so desensitized by it that we often gossip without realizing it or considering the consequences.

My wife's grandmother and her great-aunt are both in their early nineties. The godly wisdom they have contributed through the years has been invaluable to my family. They have passed on this saying that has been handed down to them from preceding generations: "If you don't have something good to say, then don't say anything at all." This maxim sums up what our reaction to gossip should be. If the church would follow this simple teaching, we would never have to worry about insulting or injuring our neighbors. Jesus summed up what God expects of His children.

One of the teachers of the law came and heard them debating. Noticing that Jesus had given them a good answer, he asked him, "Of all the commandments, which is the most important?" "The most important one," answered Jesus, "is this: 'Hear, O Israel, the Lord our God, the Lord is one. Love the Lord your God with all your heart and with all your soul and with all your mind and with all your strength.' The second is this: 'Love your neighbor as yourself.' There is no commandment greater than these."   (Mark 12:28–31)

Most people have felt the penetrating dart of gossip. Emotions generated by gossip can be extremely unsettling. Try to remember the feelings of isolation, frustration, and betrayal when somebody gossiped about you. This painful memory can be very effective in keeping you from spreading gossip's poison. The Lord wants us to prayerfully consider the feelings of others, for when we do, gossip will quickly disappear from our lips. Read what the Word says about the power of the tongue:

The tongue also is a fire, a world of evil among the parts of the body. It corrupts the whole person, sets the whole course of his life on fire, and is itself set on fire by hell. All kinds of animals, birds, reptiles and creatures of the sea are being tamed and have been tamed by man, but no man can tame the tongue. It is a restless evil, full of deadly poison.   (James 3:6–8)

One must tame the tongue before he can stop gossip, but Scripture clearly reveals man's inability to control his tongue by his own power. To control your tongue is to control your heart, and that is impossible without the indwelling power of the Holy Spirit cleansing the sinful nature. Do you gossip? Has the Lord convicted you of this practice? Then admit that you have this problem and turn to the Lord for help. Christ cannot work through you until you realize your need of Him. God's Word explains it this way:

While Jesus was having dinner at Matthew's house, many tax collectors and "sinners" came and ate with him and his disciples. When the Pharisees saw this, they asked his disciples, "Why does your teacher eat with tax collectors and 'sinners'?" On hearing this, Jesus said, "It is not the healthy who need a doctor, but the sick. But go and learn what this means: 'I desire mercy, not sacrifice.' For I have not come to call the righteous, but sinners." (Matt. 9:10–13)

The religious leaders of that day didn't recognize their need for help. They wouldn't admit their need for a Savior who could wash their sins clean. With overblown egos and zealous self-righteousness, they tried to force Jesus into their rigid religious system. Since He didn't fit, they sought to kill Him and His message. He instantly saw the pride in their hearts and essentially told them, "If you don't think I can help you, then I will help those who are sick, those who know they need help, and those who are willing to listen to Me and be changed."

Pray that God shows you the truth in this critical area of your Christian walk. If you recognize your need and turn to Jesus, you will find that His hands are outstretched in tender love to you, waiting to empower you to repent. He says to you,

Behold, I stand at the door and knock. If anyone hears My voice and opens the door, I will come in to him and dine with him, and he with Me. To him who overcomes I will grant to sit with Me on My throne, as I also overcame and sat down with My Father on His throne.
(Rev. 3:20–21 NKVJ)

Jesus Christ longs to change us into His image. His greatest desire is to have us open the doors of our hearts to Him, to willingly reveal our deepest and often darkest secrets. He wants to take what is unholy and make it holy; to transform what is evil into good; to change what is darkness into light. Only the power of God can do such miraculous feats. Only God can change gossip into grace.

Gossip is as widespread as the common cold—but much deadlier. Be honest with your Lord, for when you are, you open the door to heaven's help. Can you see yourself in the following scenario?

Ted mindlessly tapped the keyboard on his computer, inputting an endless stream of data for his government job. Glancing around the office, which held several dozen workstations, he noticed some of his coworkers staring at him. One of the ladies saw him looking her way, and she quickly turned away, stifling her laughter.

Ted knew something was going on; he just didn't know what. Struggling to overcome his sense of dread, he tried to focus on his computer screen. Seconds later, his boss stopped in front of Ted's desk.

"Hey, Ted. Do you have a minute?" asked Frank Anderson. "I'd like to see you in my office."

The frog in Ted's throat nearly silenced him. "Sh...sure, be right there."

Ted frowned as he glanced around the room. Not a soul looked at him directly as he followed the boss. Instead, as he walked past each work area, the occupants jerked around and stared at him. Their motion resembled dominoes falling one after the other. He knew it was a matter of minutes before the office gossip mill would be in full throttle. He forced a smile as he walked into Frank's office.

"I think you know why I called you here," Frank stated.

Ted tried to control the anxious feelings erupting in the pit of his stomach. Whatever this was about, from the look on Frank's face, it couldn't be good.

"Actually, Frank, I'm not sure."

Frank grimaced at the reply. Ted wasn't going to make this easy. Even though he was the boss, Frank hated confrontation.

"Well..." he stared at Ted as he sized up his guilt. "It has come to my attention that you've been looking at pornography on your computer."

Ted's eyes widened. That explained everything: the knowing looks, the mocking gestures, the lewd comments. Shocked and upset, he didn't know what to say.

"Do I take your silence as guilt? You know this is cause for dismissal."

"Guilt!" cried Ted. "Absolutely not! Where in the world did you get such an idea?"

The left side of Frank's lip twitched nervously.

"Ted, you know how gossip flies around here. Everybody seems to know about this."

Ted interrupted, "And you believe them?"

Frank motioned toward Ted as if to say, "Calm down."

"I hear more junk around here than you can possibly fathom. The serious stuff I investigate and..." He stared at Ted for several seconds, not wanting to continue the sordid story. "I found files on your computer of a pornographic nature."

Ted shook his head in disbelief. "That's impossible. You know me, Frank, and my feelings about that junk."

Frank took a deep breath as he dropped his eyes toward his desk. He scooted a piece of paper toward Ted.

"Then can you explain this?"

Ted snatched the paper off the desk and pulled it into view. Seconds later, he tossed it down, obviously annoyed by the interrogation. He glanced through the glass partitions into the surrounding offices. Every person within range of those windows was straining to hear their conversation.

Ted's demeanor changed abruptly. "Very typical." His tone confused Frank.

"Hey, try to ignore those piranhas out there."

Ted grimaced. "I'm not talking about them. The three days that those pages on the Internet were accessed—I was on vacation those days, Frank."

Frank's face turned white. It was now obvious. Whoever had looked at those pictures was the person who had spread the rumor. Suddenly, Frank smiled. He was obviously relieved by the revelation.

"I'm so sorry, Ted. I don't know how that got by me. I didn't even think about checking the dates."

Ted didn't share Frank's relief.

"'Sorry' isn't going to restore my reputation or my Christian witness out there."

"I will get to the bottom of this, Ted. I promise you that."

Ted retorted, "Even if the truth does come out, and I'm sure it will with you on it, some people would rather believe a lie."

What comes to mind when you hear that story? I think the words from my boss at the television station ring true. I asked him to tell me some words that come to his mind when he hears the word *gossip.* He said, "Revolting, sickening, vicious, infuriating, character assassination."

You can steal a person's car, and it can be replaced. You can punch someone in the gut, and the pain will diminish. You can spit in a person's face, and he can wipe the saliva away. But once you kill an individual, that life cannot be replaced. Death is permanent. Likewise, gossip is character assassination. Once an individual loses his good name, it is often impossible to get it back. It's a type of assassination that God abhors. God's Word says, *"If anyone considers himself religious and yet does not keep a tight rein on his tongue, he deceives himself and his religion is worthless"* (James 1:26).

Colossians 4:6 instructs us: *"Let your conversation be always full of grace."* Do you think that gossip and grace can coexist? Not likely. So the next time you're tempted to share something about someone else, stop and ask yourself if you are dispensing grace or gossip. In addition, refuse to listen to destructive comments about

others. As Christians, we should be busy building other people up—not tearing them down. One of the signs of a believer is that the Holy Spirit controls every part of his life—including his ears and tongue! Pray that the Holy Spirit will help you to speak words of grace. Churches are full of gossip because churches are full of lost people. Yes, even saved Christians can gossip, but they will feel guilt. They will repent, and they will seek to right the wrong they inflicted. This is the Christian way—the *"narrow...road that leads to life"* (Matt. 7:14).

Chapter Seven

Forgive and Be Forgiven

"Bear with each other and forgive whatever grievances
you may have against one another.
Forgive as the Lord forgave you."
—Colossians 3:13

Nearly all human beings, both Christians and non-Christians, have struggled to forgive. My greatest battle with unforgiveness occurred years ago. Without going through the depressing details, suffice it to say that my boss wronged me. Driving home after the incident, I thought of many clever responses to my insensitive boss—most of which would have been unacceptable in God's eyes. I wanted justice, and I wanted it now. I was fully prepared to retaliate. I was consumed with unforgiveness, bitterness, and anger. I couldn't think straight, and I couldn't pray right.

As I pulled into my driveway, I needed somebody to talk with, someone who would see *my* perspective, understand my *righteous* indignation, and feel my misery. My wife, Tina, was the perfect candidate. After all, she had had "problem" bosses before. I would tell her the entire story. I knew she would be my cheerleader for justice.

My head hung low as I shuffled through the front door and headed for the kitchen.

"Hey," I said, my voice lifeless.

Tina heard the door and turned from the kitchen counter.

"Jon, is that you?"

I mumbled, "Yeah."

I wanted her to feel sorry for me, to feel my pain.

When she saw how woebegone I looked, she stopped making dinner and hugged me.

"What in the world happened to you?"

For a moment, she expected the worse—a death in the family, some national emergency. Maybe I'd lost my job. I stared at her, weary and exhausted.

"You wouldn't believe what my boss did to me."

"What? Tell me," she said, somewhat relieved.

As I filled her in on the story, I began to sense she didn't feel my pain, my anger, my disgust. Once I finished describing every gruesome detail so that she would really appreciate the extent of my injury, she patted me on the back and smiled.

"Well, it looks like you'll have to forgive him."

I didn't expect that.

"Forgive?" I was incredulous.

She went back to dicing tomatoes. To her, the whole situation was cut-and-dried, easy to resolve.

"Yes. Forgive him. Don't you remember the situation I had with my boss? Wasn't that your advice?"

Putting words together in a complete sentence was beyond me. Tina made it sound so simple, but it wasn't! I had been wronged! Justice—okay, vengeance—must be exacted! It was easy to give godly advice, but it was another thing to take it—especially when it felt as if my world were imploding. The obvious solution, obeying God, didn't seem to be an option. A cloud of unforgiveness fogged my heart.

"But it's not that simple!" I protested. Didn't she understand what he had done to me? Where was her compassion? Why wasn't she on my side?

She stopped the dinner preparations, turned around, and placed her hands on her hips. I knew a lecture was imminent.

"Do you want to ruin your witness at work? If you don't forgive him, everyone—including your boss—will know it."

"But I do forgive him!"

She raised her eyebrows and smiled. "And I'm the Easter Bunny."

"I'm serious. You've got to understand. It's not a matter of forgiveness. I've got to work with this guy, and now I have zero respect for him."

"You don't have to respect him, Jon, but you do have to forgive him." I managed a pathetic smile before walking away. She was right, and for the average husband, that's hard to admit.

The next day at work I remember seeing my boss in his office. Did I go in there? Not on your life! When I saw his face, I instantly replayed the events from the day before. My anger and hurt rose to the surface. It took nearly a month for me to come to terms with the truth: I hadn't forgiven him. Oh, yes, I would play games with words and feelings and try to avoid the issue all together; yet, deep in my heart, I knew that a pollution as deadly as cancer was infecting my spirit.

Freedom did come, and again, it was my wife's wisdom that finally broke through Satan's chains that were binding me. I'll never forget the feeling of relief and freedom as I cried on the couch one afternoon, repenting of the unforgiveness that had taken control of my life. It was as if a thousand-pound load had been lifted off my shoulders. My fellowship with God and my relationships with my family and friends were restored, and I was free to worship the Lord again.

How did I know I had forgiven my boss? Simple! The next day at work when I looked at him, I didn't recall the wrong that he had inflicted on me. I saw him as a creation of God, not as an instrument of the devil. I saw him as a fellow human being, not a despicable man bent on my destruction. God was helping me to love him as I should.

Speaking of love, the Bible says, *"It is not rude, it is not self-seeking, it is not easily angered, it keeps no record of wrongs"* (1 Cor. 13:5). Love doesn't keep track of offenses. It doesn't recall painful wounds that people's words and actions have caused. That doesn't mean you can't remember the incident. The difference is that you don't want to! You don't keep the offense on the "front burner" of your mind. When, through the power of the Holy Spirit, love controls your life, there is no need to rehearse the wrongs you have suffered. In short, painful memories are no longer lodged like a bullet deep in your heart.

"Forgive and forget": this simple statement from a bygone era is chock-full of godly wisdom. Many people—even those who attend church regularly—are holding onto a spirit of unforgiveness. Those who are spiritually lost have the greatest disadvantage because they don't know Jesus Christ as their Savior. He is the Great Physician who can cut out the cancer of unforgiveness from our spirits, freeing us to love God and others.

One of the signs of a true Christian is the ability to forgive unconditionally. Does this mean we occasionally slip up and fall into the muddy waters of bitterness? Of course we do! But those who are saved repent of their unforgiving spirit; those who are lost don't. A life characterized and controlled by unforgiveness is a life void of God's healing power.

Want proof? Check out the Lord's Prayer.

In this manner, therefore, pray: Our Father in heaven, hallowed be Your name. Your kingdom come. Your will be done on earth as it is in heaven. Give us this day our daily bread. And forgive us our debts, as we forgive our debtors. And do not lead us into temptation, but deliver us from the evil one. For Yours is the kingdom and the power and the glory forever. Amen. (Matt. 6:9–13 NKJV)

Jesus gave us this prayer so that we would know how we should pray. Although millions of people know this prayer by heart, merely reciting it is not enough. It is a prayer that must be lived out in our lives.

The theological lessons in this prayer are tremendous, but I want to focus on only one part. Let's look at what Jesus has to say about forgiveness: *"And forgive us our debts, as we forgive our debtors"* (Matt. 6:12 NKJV). This verse alone indicates that the Lord's forgiveness of us is linked to our forgiveness of others. The two verses that follow the Lord's Prayer are amazing. They contain a message that absolutely defines Christianity to its core. Jesus didn't explain His prayer, except for the part about forgiveness. His words illuminate the blessings of forgiveness, as well as God's expectation of us to forgive one another.

> *For if you forgive men their trespasses, your heavenly Father will also forgive you. But if you do not forgive men their trespasses, neither will your Father forgive your trespasses.* (Matt. 6:14–15 NKJV)

For many who are lost in church today, this is one earth-shattering, God-fearing, boot-shaking statement. In essence, God is saying, "I cannot forgive you if you do not forgive others." People who are washed by the cleansing power of Christ's blood are forgiven. In turn, their lives are characterized by the ability to forgive those who wrong them.

If God hasn't forgiven you, how can you plan on going to heaven? God cannot and will not allow sin in His presence. He is a holy God, perfect in all His ways. Those who go to heaven must be forgiven of their sins so that they can be allowed in His Majesty's presence. When people accept Jesus as their personal Savior, their sins are transferred onto Jesus, rendering the individuals forgiven—innocent and sinless. Hence, when we reach heaven, God will not see our sins; instead, we will be clothed in His righteousness. We clearly see this picture in the book of Revelation.

> *After this I looked and there before me was a great*
> *multitude that no one could count, from every nation,*
> *tribe, people and language, standing before the throne*
> *and in front of the Lamb. They were wearing white*
> *robes and were holding palm branches in their hands.*
> (Rev. 7:9)

These *"white robes"* represent the righteousness of God that He imputes to His saints when He saves them. If we stood before Him without His forgiveness, God wouldn't see those white robes; He would see our sin, dirty and disgusting in His sight. Only forgiven people are allowed into God's glory; therefore, those who practice unforgiveness show by their actions that their salvation is fraudulent. I know these are tough words, but isn't that what the Bible says?

When Peter approached our Lord about forgiveness, his religious belief system was challenged in a big way! For a devout Jew, there was a limit on forgiveness. Once that limit had been reached, he was no longer obligated to forgive. Sure enough, Peter came to Jesus to discuss that limit. There's little doubt that Peter thought he was going to earn some brownie points with the Lord. To forgive an individual seven times showed a magnanimous spirit, yet Jesus' response revealed the smallness of Peter's spirit in regard to forgiveness.

> *Then Peter came to Jesus and asked, "Lord, how many*
> *times shall I forgive my brother when he sins against*
> *me? Up to seven times?" Jesus answered, "I tell you,*
> *not seven times, but seventy-seven times."*
> (Matt. 18:21–22)

Many in the church still sparingly mete out their forgiveness today. Somewhere deep in their hearts, they set a limit on forgiveness. Like Peter, they are unwilling to forgive beyond that mark.

This truth becomes more chilling when one considers that divorces are as common among Christians as they are among non-Christians. Marital break-ups often occur because of the couple's inability to forgive one another. The root problem in practically every divorce today can be traced to unforgiveness. Of course, circumstances, sins, personalities, and a plethora of others factors are involved; yet if one digs deeply enough, the refusal to forgive poisons the holy union. Consider the three main reasons Christian therapists list for Christian divorces: abandonment, adultery, and abuse.

What causes one person to abandon another? Why would someone resort to adultery? What is a primary cause for physical, emotional, and mental abuse? These actions are often rooted in anger, an emotion intimately tied to unforgiveness and one that everybody feels from time to time. What does the Lord say about anger? *"'In your anger do not sin': Do not let the sun go down while you are still angry"* (Eph. 4:26).

God knows we will experience anger. It's what we do with it after the feeling emerges that's of critical importance. We must deal with it, sort through the feelings and reasons for it, forgive those who caused it, and move forward in our Christian walk, free from the demonic trap set before us. If we don't deal with anger in a godly way, it will snap at us, bite us, then swallow us whole.

Ephesians 4:27 says, *"Do not give the devil a foothold."* Imagine that only a door separates you from Satan. It's closed. He's unable to get to you, and this makes you quite happy. Then you get angry with somebody, and instead of forgiving that person, you allow these angry feelings to spread unchecked within your heart and mind. Soon, that venom is circulating in your blood, making you as sick as a dog (spiritually). When you refuse to give up the anger, you've allowed the door to open ever so slightly, just enough for the devil's foot to squeeze into the door frame. So many lost in church are sweating it out, holding that door back with their own power as Satan tries to force it open. Sadly, for many, he wins the fight. Why? Satan was one of the most powerful angels created by God, and even though he fell from grace, the power he wields is as strong as ever. Satan is much stronger than carnal flesh. Only through the omnipotent power of Jesus Christ can that door be slammed in the devil's face. Only when Christ resides within you do you have a power that is greater than that of the enemy. (See 1 John 4:4.)

There is an emotional and spiritual process involved in unforgiveness. After being wronged, many react in a very predictable fashion. The process goes something like this: Disappointment breeds anger; anger breeds bitterness; bitterness breeds resentment; resentment breeds unforgiveness; unforgiveness breeds depression.

Christian therapists and their secular counterparts are swamped with patients who are completely engulfed in depression. The percentage of people who are battling depression and have unforgiveness ruling their lives is truly phenomenal. Is there a link? You bet.

Although conflict within marriages can occur for many reasons, a significant contributor to damaged relationships is the lack of forgiveness. Too many people feel they have a "right" to be unforgiving. They are, after all, the injured parties. Does the Lord's teaching on forgiveness provide an escape clause, or is everyone required to forgive those who have wronged them? Consider this scenario.

Debbie's shoulders slumped under the emotional weight she was carrying. A torrent of disappointments had washed over her like a flood, pushing her near the edge. Fearful but desperate, she had finally sought help from Steve, the associate pastor at her church and a well-respected Christian therapist.

"So can you tell me what's happening?" he asked. A Christlike peace radiated from his gentle eyes.

Debbie swallowed hard. She didn't know where to start. Pain had etched deep lines on her face.

"I'm sorry," she quietly sobbed. "Maybe I'm not ready for this."

Steve nodded. He knew how hard it must be for Debbie to seek help. He waited patiently for her to speak.

She tried again. "I'm just so sad all the time. It's like life's not worth living anymore. Everybody's letting me down," she sighed. "Even God."

Steve could feel her pain. He had seen many cases like this, and he knew that only the power of God could release her from this self-imposed dungeon imprisoning her.

"Why do you think God has let you down?"

She didn't want to think about it.

"Debbie, can you look at me?" he asked kindly.

She glanced toward him for a moment, then looked away.

"Debbie?"

She tried again. "Pastor, I'm so sorry." She began to sob.

Steve quickly responded, "It's all right, Debbie. You feel as if everybody's let you down. It's hard for you to trust anyone."

His words calmed her. She focused on his face and managed a slight smile.

"I know God hasn't let me down, but I just can't seem to shake these feelings." She wiped away the tears streaming down her face. "I can't handle this over-whelming loneliness and sadness."

Steve asked, "In other words, you're depressed?"

Through some sniffles she uttered, "Yes."

"Why do you think you're depressed?" His voice was soothing and reassuring.

"I don't know," she cried.

Pastor Steve silently prayed for God's direction as he asked, "How's your relationship with your husband? I know you've had some tough times in the past."

"That's a subject I'd rather not discuss."

"That's why we need to discuss it, Debbie. Maybe it's the reason you're feeling the way you do."

Debbie knew in her heart that he was right, but she feared looking too closely at the problem.

"Okay," she muttered barely above a whisper.

Steve's face brightened at her response.

"Your willingness to talk is a great start. Can you tell me how you feel Barry has let you down?"

The mention of her husband's name made her queasy. Their marriage of six years had degenerated into constant fights and rampant mistrust. She forced herself to speak.

"I can't stand to be around him anymore. Everything I do seems to be wrong," she cried, pausing to catch her breath. "I'm tired of all the fighting."

"What do you fight about?"

She exploded, "What don't we fight about! Money, the kids, the in-laws, sex, his job." Her face turned deadly serious. "He's not the man I married."

Steve grimaced. How he would love to say a prayer and completely restore this hurting lady, yet he knew it wasn't that easy. She was responsible to deal with the truth. He prayed that she would have the courage to do her part in restoring her marriage and her walk with the Lord.

"I'm going to ask you a very hard question, Debbie. Do I have your permission?"

Debbie hesitated, but then said, "Yes. I'm not sure I'll be able to answer it, but I'll try."

Steve was encouraged by the hint of determination he heard in her voice. He decided to dig a little deeper.

"When Barry lets you down or you two get in a fight, do you forgive him afterward?"

"Forgive him! Are you kidding? It's too late for that! Every forgiving bone in my body has been broken!"

Steve was taken aback by the vehemence in her tone.

"Do you feel as if Barry is your enemy instead of your husband and your friend?"

She sighed heavily. "Unfortunately."

Steve reached for his Bible. "I'm going to read something to you from the book of Luke: 'But I tell you who hear me: Love your enemies, do good to those who hate you, bless those who curse you, pray for those who mistreat you'" (Luke 6:27).

Debbie was visibly shaken. The Spirit of God was speaking to her, desiring to renew her spirit, but the demons taunting her wouldn't let go without a fight—a really big fight!

Steve went on to read the next verse: "If someone strikes you on one cheek, turn to him the other also. If someone takes your cloak, do not stop him from taking your tunic." Then he skipped down several verses and continued to read. "If you love those who love you, what credit is that to you? Even 'sinners' love those who love them" (v. 32).

Debbie moaned. "Pastor, I've heard those verses a hundred times. What's your point?"

Steve continued. "I want you to notice verse thirty-six. Please listen carefully." He read, *"Be merciful, just as your Father is merciful."*

He closed his Bible and looked at Debbie. The Word of God didn't seem to be improving her mood; if anything, she was more agitated.

"What do these verses mean to you, Debbie?"

She tried to think, but her emotions made it hard to be rational.

She stared at the floor as she spoke. "I don't know. Why don't you tell me?"

"Bottom line, Debbie. God says to forgive others because He forgave you, and if you don't, He won't forgive you. It's not an option; it's a command."

She slouched in her chair. Her unforgiving heart was blocking the light of God's truth. Her voice quivered from the emotional storm raging within.

"I know that I'm supposed to forgive. I just can't do it. I've tried, but you don't know how much I've been hurt."

Steve sighed at her pain.

"Of course you can't do it on your own. You have to seek God's help. Only He can enable you to forgive."

She shook her head at the thought.

"I've tried that before. It doesn't work."

Steve leaned forward, his face turning stern.

"Debbie, look at me!"

The authority in his voice jolted her. Her eyes moved slowly toward him. She felt defeated and ashamed.

"That is a lie straight from the depths of hell itself. You are believing the lies that the devil is planting inside your heart."

"But I'm a Christian. I didn't think he could do that," she countered with a confused expression.

"He can't possess you, Debbie, but you can allow him access to your life through disobedience." Steve paused for a moment, asking the Spirit for direction. "I'm going to oversimplify your situation for a moment, but I believe it will help. Then we can move forward from there."

Debbie felt a tiny spark of hope.

"Okay," began Steve, "you're in a difficult place in your marriage. For years, you haven't been forgiving your husband. Because of this, you've allowed the devil slow but sure access into your life. What do you think happens when you don't forgive?"

"Well," she shrugged her shoulders, "I guess I'm upsetting God."

He nodded without saying a word. He was hoping Debbie would really open up and see the situation through God's eyes.

"I'm not sure what you're looking for," she added, the frustration evident in her voice.

Steve placed his hands on the desk and folded them as if in prayer.

"I simply want you to be honest with God and make sure you understand His thoughts on your unforgiveness."

Her eyes scanned the room, again avoiding Steve. This was the hardest thing she had ever done. Brutal honesty before God was like heart surgery without an anesthetic.

Steve began again. "Why won't you forgive your husband, Debbie? Has he sinned against you too many times?"

Life returned to Debbie's face as she answered. "Yes. He has no right to make me feel the way he does!"

Steve turned somber at her reply.

"Debbie, I'm not saying that what your husband has done is right. But for now, let's focus on your response. Remember, your husband didn't sin just against you; he sinned against God. You're not God, and the reason you refuse to forgive him is because somewhere deep inside you, you don't understand that. It's back to the Garden of Eden again. The devil tempted Eve with the notion that she could be like God! When you refuse to forgive Barry, you are telling God that you know better than He does. When a person repents, God forgives him. He expects the same thing of us."

Though his words were pointed, his tone was gentle. The Spirit of God hovered over her as she broke into tears, years of pain and suffering spilling out. Steve sensed that the armor of pride that was separating her from God's peace was beginning to crack.

"The Bible clearly says that if we are unwilling to forgive others, then God is unwilling to forgive us." He paused, making sure she was really listening. "Debbie, Scripture clearly teaches that we must show the same forgiveness and mercy as God has shown us. It's a sign of our salvation."

Debbie's anguish deepened as the Word of God penetrated her innermost being. Steve sensed another problem he hadn't expected.

"Debbie, are you saved?"

She didn't expect his directness. She had been hiding the truth from everybody for years. Friends, family, church members—everybody simply assumed she was a Christian because she had been attending church all her life. She hoped she was born again, but deep inside her spirit, only she and the Lord knew the truth. Debbie desperately wanted to forgive Barry, yet she simply didn't have the spiritual ammunition to do it.

Suddenly, her tears stopped. She lifted her blotchy, reddened face toward the pastor and answered truthfully. "No, I'm not. I've wanted to be, but something always keeps me from doing it. I'm scared of what people will think. They believe I'm already a Christian."

He lamented to himself, *There are so many lost in the church. God, help us.* Pastor Steve was hopeful, though. He sensed that Debbie was ready to surrender all rights to herself and her unforgiveness and give them to the Lord.

"Do you want Jesus Christ to take over your life and relieve you of this pain?"

"Yes." Debbie buried her head in her hands and prayed. Years of bad decisions, personal grudges, fits of rage, and a massive amount of anger and unforgiveness peeled away from her heart. The Master Physician was in the operating room, removing every ounce of spiritual cancer in her body. Debbie's tearful prayer lasted several minutes. When she lifted her face, a new woman appeared, devoid of depression, anger, and bondage. Although she still had many difficulties ahead, she now had the power to deal with them.

Not everybody who battles unforgiveness is lost. Christians can struggle to forgive, too. But Scripture makes it perfectly clear that those who have a lifestyle of unforgiveness, anger, and bitterness do not have the Savior in their lives. Are you battling unforgiveness? Do you have intermittent victories, or have you given up trying to forgive? Do you offer a conditional forgiveness— one that says, "I forgive you this time, but if you ever do that again, I'll..."? Does that sound like Jesus to you?

Let's look at a story that Jesus told Peter and see what we can learn about the way God forgives.

Therefore, the kingdom of heaven is like a king who wanted to settle accounts with his servants. As he began the settlement, a man who owed him ten thousand talents was brought to him. Since he was not able to pay, the master ordered that he and his wife and his children and all that he had be sold to repay the debt. The servant fell on his knees before him. "Be patient with me," he begged, "and I will pay back everything." The servant's master took pity on him, canceled the debt and let him go. But when that servant went out, he found one of his fellow servants who owed him a hundred denarii. He grabbed him and began to choke him. "Pay back what you owe me!" he demanded. His fellow servant fell to his knees and begged him, "Be patient with me, and I will pay you back." But he refused. Instead, he went off and had the man thrown into prison until he could pay the debt. When the other servants saw what had happened, they were greatly distressed and went and told their master everything that had happened. Then the master called the servant in. "You wicked servant," he said, "I canceled all that debt of yours because you begged me to. Shouldn't you have had mercy on your fellow servant just as I had on you?" In anger his master turned him over to the jailers to be tortured, until he should pay back all he owed. This is how my heavenly Father will treat each of you unless you forgive your brother from your heart.

(Matt. 18:23–35)

When the first servant was called before the king, his debt was more than he could ever pay. In modern terms, it would equate to several million dollars. So he did the only thing he could—he dropped to his knees and begged for his life! He didn't have the option of bankruptcy; most debtors at this time were sold into slavery until the money was paid back. What a picture this story is of God's mercy! Our debt is so immense! We can never pay, atone for, or make up in any way for our sins. Just as this servant dropped to his knees before the king, we must come to the Cross in true humility. We must fall on our faces, admitting our need for a Savior, understanding that we cannot get to heaven on our own merit.

Jesus Christ is ready and willing to "take pity" on any person who is willing to admit his sins and be ready to repent of them. The individual in this parable apparently did just that; yet immediately after experiencing God's loving forgiveness, he quickly found a person in need of his forgiveness but refused to follow through in like fashion.

At best, we could say this individual was ungrateful; at worst, he was completely unfazed and unchanged by his encounter with the king. The money owed him by his fellow servant would amount to only a few dollars in our currency. In other words, this person's debt was so small that it was a minor offense that even a worldly minded person could easily forgive. However, instead of showing mercy, the ungrateful servant took justice into his own hands and demanded restitution.

Notice the response of the other servants to this man's lack of forgiveness. They were *"greatly distressed"* (Matt. 13:31). True disciples of God know what He expects of them and when somebody comes along whose behavior reflects poorly on Christ and His church, it grieves them. Surely people had heard of how merciful the king had been to this servant, and you can rest assured they were watching this man's every move. To put it bluntly, this unforgiving servant was making God look bad. God jealously guards His reputation, for without it, nobody would seek Him.

Don't think that the world isn't watching us. We have received immeasurable mercy from our King's hand. What does it do to God's good name when we treat His gift with such disdain and act like a merciless servant? Have you heard comments like these from non-believers?

- I don't get it. Susan's been mad at me for weeks. She talks about how Christians should forgive, but she sure doesn't do it herself.
- I used to think Bob was so religious, but not anymore. He's can hold a grudge with the best of them.
- I don't think Alex likes me anymore. Ever since we got into that disagreement a couple of months ago, he won't even talk to me.
- Have you seen how Sheila treats her husband? She's all over his case every time I see them together. I'm glad she's not my wife.

Every one of these situations is rooted in unforgiveness. It grieves God's heart when we refuse to show the same mercy to others that He has shown to us. People see this unloving behavior and wonder why Christians aren't practicing what the Bible teaches. You've probably heard this statement before, but it's worth repeating: You may be the only God some people see. Don't miss the chance to show others what He is really like; maximize your opportunities to let His forgiving love shine through you.

The story doesn't end with the fellow servants being upset. No, they went to the king and told him everything that had happened. The Bible says that the king was angry, and he punished the *"wicked"* man by turning him over to jailers who would torture him until he could pay his debts. You understand how long his sentence was, don't you? His unforgiving actions resulted in a lifetime of torture and imprisonment!

You can be the most gifted Sunday school teacher of all time, you can know the Bible inside and out, you can fill a position of leadership within the church—but if you don't love and forgive your neighbor, then you're not practicing the most basic tenet of Christianity. The foundation to almost every other Christian gift is love. If you're not forgiving, you're not loving. As Paul wrote,

If I speak in the tongues of men and of angels, but have not love, I am only a resounding gong or a clanging cymbal. If I have the gift of prophecy and can fathom all mysteries and all knowledge, and if I have a faith that can move mountains, but have not love, I am nothing. If I give all I possess to the poor and surrender my body to the flames, but have not love, I gain nothing....And now these three remain: faith, hope and love. But the greatest of these is love. (1 Cor. 13:1–3, 13)

Why does an unforgiving spirit anger our Lord? Picture a couple who has been married several years. Every day, Brenda does dozens of wonderful things for her husband. Alan, on the other hand, does absolutely nothing for his wife. He takes and takes and takes, completely absorbed in his own life. How long will it be before Brenda questions his love for her? She shows her love by the things she does for him; he shows his lack of love by the things he doesn't do.

Similarly, God forgives thousands upon thousands of sins that we have committed. He's always there for us—twenty-four hours a day, seven days a week. His love for us is unconditional. So here's the ten-thousand-dollar question: What have we done for Him? Have we shown Him our gratitude by extending mercy to others? Forgiving those who have hurt us pleases God immensely. It honors His good name and leads others to seek His forgiveness.

Although God loves us so much and wants to forgive us, He is not soft on sin. Let's get serious about the consequences of unforgiveness. Just as the king in the parable turned the unforgiving servant over to the torturers, those who are perpetually unforgiving will reap the same disastrous consequences. This truth does not generate the warm fuzzies. It isn't popular with the "God is love" crowd, but let's not miss the point of this story. Those who don't forgive will not receive forgiveness themselves, and they will pay an eternal price for their unforgiveness.

Who is the unforgiving servant? First, he can represent the Christian who is having a problem with forgiveness. Sometimes God allows the devil to cause His children misery for a season in order to bring them to repentance through the trials they go through. Few things are more torturous than bitterness, rage, depression, and unforgiveness ruling in a person's heart. Because God loves us so much, He will go to great lengths to reconcile us to Himself. He can even "use" the enemy's attacks to our good—to wake us out of our spiritual slumber. His Holy Spirit is faithful to convict us of our sins. When the believer responds to the Spirit and repents, he is drawn into close fellowship once again with God. It is not an easy process, but it works.

The unforgiving servant also can represent the lost in church who are ruled by unforgiveness. God's heart aches for these individuals. They assume they are Christians because they attend church, and they try to be good, but they have never asked Jesus to come into their hearts—and meant it. They have never confessed their sins and trusted in Him as their Savior. Their ongoing lack of love and forgiveness is proof of their unregenerate hearts. These people are the hardest for God to reach, but what is impossible with man, is possible with God.

Unforgiveness is nothing to play around with! Since the servant would never be able to pay back his debts, his torture would continue forever. Likewise, those who never receive the gift of salvation but try to atone for their sins through a lifetime of good works will never come close to paying for their debt of sin. Because they refuse to seek forgiveness from the Savior and, in turn, to show mercy to others, their torture will be everlasting. This is not a new concept but an age-old truth that has lost some popularity in a modern, feel-good church.

Is there someone in your life whom you refuse to forgive? Is there anyone you will not talk to? Are you holding a long-standing grudge? Do you feel so wronged by

someone that you maintain your "right" not to forgive? If Stephen could forgive those who stoned him, if Christ forgave those who crucified Him, what is our excuse for an unforgiving spirit?

Of how much have you been forgiven? Do you have a limit on what you will forgive? God's grace and power is ready to flow through every Christian who calls on His name. Unforgiveness is a roadblock of man-made stone that God will not tear down without your approval.

When I was a child, I liked to tie a string around my forefinger and watch the blood flow stop. In a similar way, unforgiveness constricts the Spirit's blood flow to your heart. Without the blood, there is no life, no peace, and no forgiveness. If unforgiveness is robbing you of life, release your pain and anger to Jesus. Experience the joy of forgiving and being forgiven.

Chapter Eight

A Seared Conscience

"I strive always to keep my conscience clear
before God and man."
—Acts 24:16

Calvin sighed as he tossed his overloaded suitcase on the bed. He was growing weary of these weeklong business trips. Ever since he had taken this consulting job last year, he spent nearly every week on the road, away from his wife and kids. Although he looked forward to being with them on weekends, the time was usually filled with catching up on household responsibilities. They hardly had any quality time together anymore. By Sunday afternoon, he was preparing to leave again and already slipping back into business mode.

His work kept him busy twelve to fourteen hours a day. There was little time for relaxation or personal pleasure. Although Calvin had been a Christian for years, missing mid-week prayer meetings and too many Sunday services had begun to take its toll on his spiritual life.

Lately, he had found himself relieved when his work schedule kept him from church. Ever since the new pastor had come, he hadn't enjoyed being there. The pastor's messages were too judgmental, in Calvin's opinion. Each time he walked into the sanctuary, guilt convicted him. He was relieved when he could escape and focus on work. At least the guilty feelings subsided then. Calvin didn't like being told what to do. He trusted in his own ability to make decisions. He didn't want anyone interfering in his business.

He plopped down on the hard bed and grabbed the remote control. He positioned both pillows behind his back.

"That's better," he mumbled.

He hit the power button, ready to relax. He had the rest of the night to himself. The buttons on the remote control responded to his every whim. It took less than a minute for him to fly through a maze of channels, finding them all boring and unfulfilling. Then the cable box on top of the television caught his eye.

"That's more like it."

He got up off the bed and walked over to the television. He scanned the directions for a moment, directions he was all too familiar with.

A thrill went through him as he saw the listing: Adult Movies. He enjoyed the images those words brought to his mind. His life had become dull. He needed some excitement to spice things up, to keep him going. He rationalized his behavior by telling himself he wasn't a bad person. He had never solicited a prostitute or had an affair. It was all innocent entertainment, a needed distraction and release. After all, it made him feel better. It helped him deal with his frustrations.

Lately, it seemed as if his wife didn't understand his needs. In his opinion, he was a good husband, a loving father, and a decent Christian. Calvin figured he was going through a mid-life crisis—not a spiritual battle. For a moment, he thought about his wife. Then he pushed those thoughts aside. She wasn't here, and what she didn't know wouldn't hurt her.

Calvin maneuvered through the on-screen commands. Then he repositioned himself on the bed and placed his hands behind his head.

He thought, Maybe this life isn't so bad, after all. Nobody's making demands on me. I have the evening to do what I want.

The Holy Spirit spoke to his heart, but Calvin wasn't listening. His once tender conscience had become hardened to the Spirit's voice. It had been seared through repeated disobedience. Once again, Calvin quenched the Spirit as he sought to fulfill the lusts of his flesh.

Sin is seductive. Too many are numbed by its effects and unwittingly destroyed. Like a sheep dragged away by a hungry lion, they are ripped apart by the devil who is bent on destroying God's creation.

> *The Spirit clearly says that in later times some will abandon the faith and follow deceiving spirits and things taught by demons. Such teachings come through hypocritical liars, whose consciences have been seared as with a hot iron.* (1 Tim. 4:1–2)

If one hundred people lost in church today were to be gathered together and questioned, one shocking truth would quickly emerge. They don't have a Spirit-sensitized conscience! They may go through the motions of being a Christian and sit in the pews faithfully each Sunday, but they are not living in close fellowship with the Lord and seeking the Spirit's guidance on a daily basis.

The Bible speaks of the straight and narrow road that few find. Of course, this describes salvation, but this road can be traveled only when the conscience has the ability to hear from its Guide.

Our consciences are given to us by God. Human beings are born with a sense of right and wrong. The Scripture says,

> *Indeed, when Gentiles, who do not have the law, do by nature things required by the law, they are a law for themselves, even though they do not have the law, since they show that the requirements of the law are*

written on their hearts, their consciences also bearing
witness, and their thoughts now accusing, now even
defending them. (Rom. 2:14–15)

Paul was not saying that the Gentiles had the law written on their hearts. No, that can happen only when we repent and know Christ as Savior. The Spirit-led conscience is the product of a personal relationship with the Lord. But the Gentiles did have a knowledge of the law, though that alone is not enough to save. Religiously following external rules of conduct will not substitute for holiness of heart.

Yet God instills a conscience in every human being, which is a gift of grace. What we call the conscience, theologians have termed "preventing or prevenient grace." The Spirit is at work from the start. That's why we feel guilty when we do something we know we shouldn't do. But how do we know what is right or wrong in the first place? Simply put, it is the work of the Spirit, who awakens us to the obvious difference between what we do and what we understand that we should do. Left to our own consciences, we would all cry with Paul,

> *I do not understand what I do. For what I want to do I*
> *do not do, but what I hate I do....I know that nothing*
> *good lives in me, that is, in my sinful nature. For I have*
> *the desire to do what is good, but I cannot carry it out.*
> *For what I do is not the good I want to do; no, the evil I*
> *do not want to do—this I keep on doing....What a*
> *wretched man I am! Who will rescue me from this body*
> *of death?* (Rom. 7:15, 18–19, 24)

What is the only remedy for this dilemma? It is to pray and ask Jesus to come into your life and forgive your sins. Receive His gift of freedom from condemnation. Only He can set you *"free from the law of sin and death"* (Rom. 8:2). When a person becomes a Christian, the Holy Spirit fills his heart and makes his conscience

Spirit-sensitized. Under the control of the Holy Spirit, the conscience helps the Christian to walk in the ways of the Lord. When Jesus comes into your life, He cleans house, purging the stain of sin that's polluting you. He makes you a *"new creation"* (2 Cor. 5:17), with new priorities, attitudes, and values.

Those lost in church have some form of conscience, but it doesn't resemble a Spirit-sensitized conscience. When asked why they don't listen to their consciences, they may say something like this:

- What do you mean? I do listen to my conscience.
- Oh, come on. I'm not perfect, but nobody is.
- God understands my weaknesses.
- I can do things that I used to think were wrong because I am more mature in my faith now.

Something lacking in many churches today is accountability. Confessing sin to one another is a foundation and pillar of New Testament Christianity. It's a sign of repentance, brokenness, and openness—qualities that accompany salvation. If a person lost in church is confronted with his lack of commitment, lack of fruit, lack of love, and lack of conscience, this is what you may hear:

- Who are you to judge me?
- It's none of your business how I live my life.
- I'll let my conscience be my guide. I didn't ask for your opinion anyway.

First Samuel 25:31 speaks of a guilty conscience creating a *"staggering burden"* upon a person's heart. Those who haven't given their hearts to the Lord often feel this immense yoke as they return to church week after week, unchanged. For many of the religious lost, this spiritual load of culpability is so deeply ingrained, they don't recognize it as guilt at all. Yes, they are depressed, worn-out, down about life, and generally unhappy, but they don't recognize the truth of their condition. Instead of facing facts, they make excuses. Instead of turning to God, they turn to poor substitutes.

Some seek relief from guilt through the misuse of prescription drugs. Too many doctors are more than willing to prescribe mind- and emotion-altering drugs to relieve the symptoms of a guilty conscience. Although not all depression is rooted in anger and unforgiveness, Christian therapists recognize the frequent connection between the two. Sometimes medication is the appropriate course to take. Sadly, though, many people in the church turn to drugs first instead of God. Yet only He can remove the burden of guilt and remove our sins from us, *"as far as the east is from the west"* (Ps. 103:12).

Others seek fulfillment through unhealthy relationships. God desires a deep, intimate, honest relationship with His children. When the lost in church lose their connection with God through damaged consciences, many turn to idolatrous relationships to fill their God-shaped vacuum. Single people may turn to those who offer sex without moral constraints. Married people may have affairs that offer only a fleeting satisfaction. Teenagers may do everything they can to belong to the "in" crowd, seeking to live life for the moment and not for eternity. Others spend their time with friends who give them worldly advice that further decimates their spiritual condition. Proverbs offers godly insight on who you should and shouldn't spend your time with:

> *Do not make friends with a hot-tempered man, do not associate with one easily angered, or you may learn his ways and get yourself ensnared.* (Prov. 22:24–25)

> *He who walks with the wise grows wise, but a companion of fools suffers harm.* (Prov. 13:20)

> *He who keeps the law is a discerning son, but a companion of gluttons disgraces his father.* (Prov. 28:7)

A man who loves wisdom brings joy to his father, but a companion of prostitutes squanders his wealth.

(Prov. 29:3)

Here's the bottom line: Don't trust in what mankind can do for you; instead, trust in God! He's all you need for health, wisdom, and happiness. Psalm 118:8 reminds us, *"It is better to take refuge in the LORD than to trust in man."*

Some people do not resort to drugs or bad relationships to ease their guilty consciences. Instead, they turn to Eastern religions and cults to satisfy their appetites and soothe their pain. They easily fall for a worldly philosophy because they are not well grounded in the truth of God's Word. God is not pleased with those who pursue vain philosophies that masquerade as spiritual enlightenment. Proverbs 1:27–33 clearly states,

> *When calamity overtakes you like a storm, when disaster sweeps over you like a whirlwind, when distress and trouble overwhelm you. Then they will call to me but I will not answer; they will look for me but will not find me. Since they hated knowledge and did not choose to fear the LORD, since they would not accept my advice and spurned my rebuke, they will eat the fruit of their ways and be filled with the fruit of their schemes. For the waywardness of the simple will kill them, and the complacency of fools will destroy them; but whoever listens to me will live in safety and be at ease, without fear of harm.*

Unaware of the danger, uninformed Christians may embrace New Age beliefs. Proverbs 28:26 clearly warns against this humanistic thinking: *"He who trusts in himself is a fool."* An honest assessment of our lives without Christ can be summed up in one word: *hopeless.* Trying to run our own lives is like setting a two-year-old child loose to do what he wants with no guidance or telling an automobile to fix itself or expecting a dog to train itself without its master's direction. The conscience cannot look to itself for advice; it must rely on its Maker and Programmer, God Almighty.

Pondering his next move, Peter anxiously ran his hands through his prematurely graying hair. His wife Kathy sat across the kitchen table from him, sharing in his misery. They were desperate and clueless. Their only child, Samantha, was, in short, a terror! She was six years old with fire-engine red hair and a red-hot attitude to match. Peter and Kathy watched their daughter playing outside. They prayed for the day when seeing her would bring joy—not heartache and frustration.

"I say we go see a doctor about this. Maybe she should be on some kind of medication."

Kathy looked like she'd just come through a war zone. Endless nights with interrupted sleep and fighting battles with her child each day had taken a toll on her. She wished she could run far away and start over again.

Kathy cried, "I'm not putting my daughter on drugs! There's got to be a better answer."

Peter shook his head in frustration. "Well, that's great! What do you suggest? Do you have any more bright ideas?"

His sarcastic tone irritated Kathy. "Give me a break! You're the one who suggested letting her have her way!"

Peter shot back, "And you're the one who coddles her every time I try to discipline her."

Kathy started to answer, but stopped. She knew they were both to blame. She felt helpless as she watched their unruly daughter play outside in the backyard. She couldn't believe the pain a child could cause. It was as if Samantha had no conscience. Kathy recalled a Bible verse from Proverbs 10:1 that they had read in last night's Bible study: *"A wise son brings joy to his father, but a foolish son grief to his mother."* She burst into tears, her head falling to the table, her heart sinking to the floor.

Peter hesitated to console her. The constant struggle to discipline Samantha was affecting their marriage. He knew that Samantha also was hurting. He slowly reached toward Kathy and placed his hands over hers.

"Hey, it's going to be fine, honey." His hollow eyes betrayed his lack of confidence. "It's all going to work out. We'll find a way somehow."

Kathy's sobbing continued. Just then, the doorbell rang.

"Don't answer it!" begged Kathy, tears streaking down her cheeks.

Peter pulled away. "I've got to, sweetie. I'm expecting an important package."

Kathy was livid. "How can you think of work at a time like this!"

Peter stopped in the middle of the hallway. His hands were shaking. His temper was reaching the boiling point.

"You..." He stopped the venom at the last second. Peter walked to the door and put on a pretense of well-being before opening it. Outside was their good friend Willy.

"Hey, brother, what's going on?" asked Willy, his contagious smile reaching out to Peter.

Peter let down his guard.

"Hey, Willy." He shrugged his shoulders and listened for Kathy's cries. He didn't hear anything.

"Come on in. Things aren't going too well."

Willy sensed the demonic cloud in the house, and he immediately started to pray.

"That's why I'm here, Peter. I was hoping to talk to you and Kathy about Samantha."

"I don't understand," Peter responded. "Has she done something we should know about?"

Willy put his arm around Peter as they walked toward the kitchen. He smiled at Kathy as she tried to put on her best face. Clearly, she was annoyed at the interruption. Peter pulled out a chair for him.

"Our little ones play together a lot. We've noticed that Samantha's been pretty defiant lately."

Kathy quickly dried her eyes and said, "I'm so sorry. Has she hurt Destiny? Do you want us to keep her away from your house?"

Willy's kind smile comforted Kathy.

"No, it's not that. We all love little Samantha."

Kathy was relieved. She didn't want to lose close friends over Samantha's behavior.

"Well, then, what is it?" Kathy asked.

For a moment or two, it appeared Willy was at a loss for words. He didn't want to hurt their feelings, and he certainly didn't want to lose them as friends. But he knew that the Lord had led him here to talk with them today. He recalled a Bible verse from Proverbs 9:8: *"Rebuke a wise man and he will love you."* That encouragement from the Word invigorated him.

"Guys, I'm just going to lay it out on the table."

Kathy's eyes widened. Willy's directness surprised her. He was usually so easygoing.

Peter nudged him on the shoulder with a gentle fist.

"Give it to us straight! Do you have a word from the Lord?"

Willy wanted to beat around the bush, but the Spirit of God wouldn't let him.

"When Samantha is at our house, she doesn't seem to listen very well. It's starting to confuse Destiny."

Kathy's emotions were on edge.

"I'm so sorry, Willy. We're really working with her, but nothing seems to help."

Willy's smile was genuine.

"I know how hard you two are trying to raise Samantha the right way. I was hoping to share something we've learned with Destiny—something that's really helped her learn to be obedient."

Willy's meek approach calmed them. They trusted him and were willing to hear any advice he might have.

Peter responded, "Hey, if it's worked for you guys," he looked at Kathy, "then we're all ears."

Kathy added, "Destiny is so well-behaved. How do you two do it?"

Willy was overjoyed by their reaction. He and his wife Debra had been praying for wisdom over this situation.

"I can sum it up in one word: *conscience.*"

"I think God forgot to put one in Samantha," Kathy said, half-jokingly.

Willy chuckled, but Peter didn't. As her father, he hated to admit he'd had the same doubts about his own child.

"God places a conscience in each of us," Willy said. He sighed as he looked out the window. "But it does seem some children are more difficult than others."

"You can say that again," moaned Peter.

"God has taught us that it's our responsibility to develop that God-given conscience within Destiny. Left to herself, she wouldn't listen to it most of the time. It's our job as parents to teach her right from wrong."

Kathy knew where he was going. She confessed, "I'm a terrible parent. I knew it. It's all my fault!"

Willy continued, "No, Kathy. It won't help to blame yourself. We've taken a course at our church about parenting. And let me tell you," he chuckled, "we were doing so many things wrong with Destiny. The big things we learned are to be consistent and not to be lazy. In other words, teach your child to obey, and don't overlook any rebellion."

Peter and Kathy stared at each other for a long while. They were doing the exact opposite, giving up when Samantha bucked them and ignoring all but her greatest offenses.

"So what you're saying is," Peter replied, "go to war and take no prisoners."

Willy laughed. "I can promise you it will be a war at first, but after that, the hourly battles will subside. She may test you for years to come, but the rebellion will lessen. There will be times between episodes for you to catch your breath before the next outburst."

Kathy appeared relieved by his words. They needed support from somebody other than each other.

"You pegged it, Willy," admitted Kathy. She looked at Peter with a rather large smile, something that had been missing for months. "We've all but given up. What's the best way to start?"

Willy was delighted.

"Again, it all begins with the conscience. You two have to help rebuild it so that Samantha not only knows the difference between right and wrong, but also wants to obey. It's going to take a lot of prayer, tears, and consistent effort on both your parts. The key is to recognize that you are in charge."

His face was dead serious. He paused to let the truth sink in. Lately, Samantha had been the one in charge.

"God has given you the responsibility to help her make the right decisions. As she learns to submit to your authority, it will be easier for her to one day submit to the Lord's authority. When you teach her to obey, you are strengthening her conscience. You need to teach her heart to react to God's commands. As she learns to love and trust you, one day she will understand that God, her heavenly Father, wants her to completely love and trust Him with her life."

Willy's words energized Peter. He practically jumped out of his seat and went to the back door. Seconds later, Willy and Kathy watched him approach Samantha.

"Samantha, come in right now. I need to talk to you."

Samantha pretended not to hear him. She was having fun playing with her dolls. She was not about to be bothered by her dad.

Normally, Peter would have kept yelling until Samantha got tired of hearing him and acquiesced. Peter turned around and winked at Kathy and Willy before he started toward Samantha with a new sense of wisdom and purpose. He wasn't about to let his precious child destroy herself. He was going to intervene now...before she was a teenager and totally out of control. If he didn't break her rebellious spirit now, he didn't even want to think what she would be like as a young adult. He wanted what was best for his child, and he knew that God wanted that, too.

Speaking to Samantha in a gentle but firm voice, he said, "I expect you to listen to me the first time." He picked her up off the ground. The look on her face was comical. For a moment, she was angry, but as he carried her into the house explaining the new ground rules that would be strictly enforced, a smile emerged on her face.

"God is going to be the boss in this house from now on. He's put your mother and me in charge, and He expects us to make you obey no matter what. Do you understand?"

She quickly responded, "Yes, Daddy."

Her obedience stunned him.

"Why are you smiling at me like that?"

Samantha's little-girl answer cut him in two.

"Because you remind me of Mr. Willy."

How does a conscience become seared? Every minute of every hour—day in, day out—we have a choice to make: Will we obey God or not? Either we obey Him and are blessed, or we disobey and suffer the consequences. When we obey God and the conscience He gave us, we are building up our spiritual immune system against further demonic attacks. When we disobey, we slowly dull God's voice inside us and deplete the spiritual antibodies that protect us. I'm using a medical analogy to make an important point here: The spiritual and the physical have some very similar characteristics. This correlation is not by mistake! The Creator designed the physical, mental, and spiritual realms to work in harmony.

Doctors warn their patients about certain symptoms to watch for before a life-threatening heart attack hits. Those who ignore the warning signs are often the ones killed by this catastrophic event. If these signs are ignored for too long, the damage is often irreversible.

One can easily see the parallel with the conscience. When we refuse to listen to it, we are setting ourselves up for trouble. The early warning signs that indicate a problem in the body can be likened to the voice of our conscience that urges us to use caution or to avoid some situation. God is a compassionate God; He warns us, but it's up to us to listen and obey.

The great hurricane of 1900 destroyed the port city of Galveston, Texas. It was one of the worst natural disasters ever to strike America. Thousands lost their lives; tens of thousands lost everything but their lives. There were two subtle warnings of the impending monster, but only those with an expertise in weather could read them. The waves were unusually large and building, and the barometer was plummeting faster than anybody could remember. If everybody in that doomed town could have read the signs from nature, they could have fled inland and been saved. And if everybody could read the spiritual barometer called the conscience and recognize the towering waves of guilt slamming into their hearts, they could avoid the self-inflicted destructive storms of life.

A volcano generally gives out warning signs before it erupts. Smoke billowing from the crater, a buildup of lava, and minor earthquakes around the mountain often foreshadow deadly explosions. Many living near rumbling volcanoes find it inconvenient to evacuate, and merely hope its bark doesn't translate into a bite. Similarly, the conscience sends its own signals, namely guilt, hoping to rouse an individual from spiritual slumber. All too often we find it inconvenient to listen to the warnings because they call for changes that will jar us from our comfort zones.

Can you sear your conscience beyond repair? It may reach a point where you can no longer help yourself, but God is able to restore a damaged conscience. Look at this encouraging word from Matthew 19:26: *"With God all things are possible."*

Jesus Christ can fix anything! An individual can drive God out of his life and ignore his conscience to the point where it is damaged, but God will do anything and everything to bring us back into close fellowship with Him. Yet we are responsible for seeking God's face, for admitting and repenting of our sins, and for coming into the fellowship of believers once again. If a person rejects God's discipline and refuses to listen to the voice of his conscience, only God Almighty knows the outcome. Hebrews 10:26–27 states:

> *If we deliberately keep on sinning after we have received the knowledge of the truth, no sacrifice for sins is left, but only a fearful expectation of judgment and of raging fire that will consume the enemies of God.*

Hebrews 10:31 also warns, *"It is a dreadful thing to fall into the hands of the living God."* Repent before it's too late. Salvation and repentance go together. God wants every Christian to be like the apostle Paul, who said, *"My conscience is clear"* (1 Cor. 4:4).

Where are you in your Christian walk? Can you say that your conscience is clear? Are you hearing from God through your conscience? A great way to assess your Christian walk is to examine your conscience. Ask the Lord to mold and shape your conscience, to give you the power to obey it, and the desire to do so.

Many lost in church are confused with matters of the conscience. They say, "I listen to my conscience!" This may be true. But unless the Holy Spirit indwells your heart and convicts you, your conscience often misleads you. Allow God to have full control of your life, and He will guide you in the paths of righteousness.

The tenth chapter of the book of John tells us that God's sheep hear His voice and obey Him. Are you hearing God's commands through your conscience? If not, ask the Lord why you can no longer hear His voice. It is God's desire to speak to you. That's why He sent the Holy Spirit to be our Counselor—to live in us and be with us forever. (See John 14:16–17.)

Chuck dropped into his favorite leather chair, canvassing the hundreds of tax documents strewn across his desk. It was the middle of February and bitterly cold outside. Only the birds had been smart enough to escape to the South. The kids were driving him crazy from being cooped up in the house, and his boss was demanding that he work overtime with no extra pay. His worn, bloodshot eyes tiredly scanned the disaster before him. *Taxes are as irritating as ingrown toenails,* he thought. Discouraged and frustrated, he dreamed of a tropical vacation with no snow, no irate boss, no kids, and—most of all—no taxes.

"Honey," called his wife from downstairs in the kitchen. "Can you take the trash out? I've got garlic in there, and it's—"

Chuck interrupted, "Okay, okay. Just give me a couple of minutes." He stared at the paper pile and muttered, "Or a couple of years."

Chuck had been an avid churchgoer for more than ten years. He had been saved while in his mid-twenties and had always been deeply committed to his Christian principles. After they married and three kids came along, life became more complicated. His time with the Lord was sporadic, at best. The worries of the world were crowding out his devotional life, leaving him depressed and burdened with anxiety. It used to be easy to know the Lord's will and direction for his life, but now, it was a long shot to say the least.

The door cracked open. "How long are you going to be doing that?" questioned his wife, Wanda.

Chuck abruptly turned to face her. "As long as it takes!" He spoke louder than he intended, annoyed by the interruption.

Wanda squelched the sarcastic reply that came to mind. Her relationship with the Lord had really grown this past year. She knew that the time she spent studying the Bible, her new regimen of fasting, and her daily prayer times were making the difference.

"Sorry I disturbed you, sweetheart. Just wanted you to know that dinner will be ready in thirty minutes."

Her gentle reply sent waves of guilt through Chuck. He pushed the guilt aside and turned back to the paperwork. The Holy Spirit urged him to go after her and apologize, but his conscience ignored the Spirit's promptings.

"I'm so fed up with these taxes!" he vented. He looked around the desktop for a pen. "The government has no right to demand so much of me! They're wasting half of what they take from me anyway."

Chuck grabbed the 1040 form and stared at the multiple lines of mumbo-jumbo and legalese. He placed the document in front of him and reached for the instruction book that resembled an encyclopedia. As he flipped through the pages and fine print, his eyes blurred. Minutes later, he threw it on the floor and cursed.

"They steal all this money from me—and now they want to steal all my free time, too!"

Turning back to the 1040 form in front of him, he copied his gross income from his W-2. Once he finished the first couple of lines, he turned his attention toward the mountain of forms and receipts to his left and right. Painstakingly, he began to arrange them in an order that coincided with the schedules to which they applied.

"Twenty minutes to dinner," called his wife.

Frustration overwhelmed him. This dizzying work was the last thing he wanted to do. Suddenly, an idea planted from below sprouted in his heart. He didn't fight it or question it; he simply obeyed. He jumped out of the swivel chair and hurried to the closet, stepping on a couple of misplaced toys along the way. He grabbed last year's tax form as if it were his salvation and ran back to the desk, missing the toys this time around. He copied all the numbers from last year, adding a little bit extra for each of the deductions. It took less than fifteen minutes. He quickly signed his name and casually tossed the finished but fraudulent document against the keyboard of his computer.

He squashed the momentary feelings of guilt. He started to walk down the stairs but suddenly stopped. He cursed under his breath and went back into his office to grab the tax forms. With papers in hand, he nonchalantly strolled downstairs. The scent of fried chicken permeated the house, causing his lingering doubts to vanish. He walked into the kitchen and kissed Wanda on the cheek.

"Mm, mm, that smells heavenly!"

"Thanks! And you won't believe what's for dessert."

"What?"

"It's a surprise!"

Chuck reacted like a toddler denied his favorite toy.

"Ah, come one! Don't do that to me," he whined.

Wanda smiled. "Okay. It's chocolate cake with chocolate frosting and chocolate swirls—your favorite!"

Chuck kissed her on the cheek.

"You're the best." He placed the tax form on the counter. "Sign here."

Wanda looked at the form and then at him.

"I thought it would take hours for you to finish that!"

Chuck hesitated for a moment. He wasn't about to tell her the truth. She didn't have to be bothered with such trivial matters.

"Oh, you misunderstood. I was referring to the state return. The federal one was easy," he lied, congratulating himself for his quick thinking.

Wanda took the pen and signed her name. She didn't bother to look at the return; she trusted Chuck unconditionally.

How trustworthy is your conscience? Have your convictions changed over the years? Do you watch movies or read books that once you would have judged to be inappropriate? Do you justify actions that before you would have repented over? As human beings, we are awfully good at rationalizing our behaviors. We can become so desensitized to sin that we no longer recognize it for what it is.

Have you heard the lesson of the frog? It is said that if you put a frog into boiling water, it will hop out to safety right away. But if you put a frog in tepid water and gradually turn up the heat, it will not be aware of the threat in time—and will boil to death.

Keep your conscience tender. Ask the Holy Spirit to renew your mind and to increase your ability to recognize His still, small voice. Be sensitive to the Spirit, and He will keep you out of hot water.

The story is told of a man who went door to door in a village, telling the people at each house, "Flee! All is discovered!" The most unlikely members of the community took off running. Obviously, they had guilty consciences. What would happen if someone came to your door and said, "Your secrets are revealed!" Would you look for a place to hide? One day we will all stand before the One who knows everything about us. Unless we have exchanged our guilt for His righteousness, we will stand condemned. Seek His forgiveness, and walk in His ways. Then you will hear the blessed words, *"Well done, good and faithful servant!"* (Matt. 25:21).

Do you have a clear conscience? If not, the good news is that you can. Sin hardens the conscience, but Christ can restore it and make it tender once more. *"Today, if you hear his voice, do not harden your hearts"* (Heb. 3:15).

Chapter Nine

False Prophet or Faithful Shepherd?

*"Do not believe every spirit, but test the spirits to see
whether they are from God, because many false prophets
have gone out into the world."*
—1 John 4:1

Many who are lost in church have more than themselves to blame. Within various denominations scattered across the globe, people are being misled by preachers, prophets, and priests who are not anointed by the Holy Spirit to preach God's Word. Although these churchgoers may feel secure in their walk with the Lord, they are being taught half-truths and outright lies by those who should know better. In this chapter, we will explore how to recognize false prophets, God's attitude toward them, and what to do when we encounter them. We also will look at several deceptions they propagate.

Imagine you're driving down an old country road, enjoying the scenic landscape. It's a sunshiny day. Your windows are down, and a gentle breeze blows through your hair. Suddenly, you notice a black and orange sign with these words written on it: "Warning—Do Not Enter." On the bottom right is a symbol of a car enclosed in a circle. Over the picture is a diagonal black line. You've never seen this kind of sign before. You're sure you are on the right road, but you slow down momentarily. Seeing no physical barriers blocking the road, you decide to proceed. You travel a mile or so at full speed, and then you see it.

The road is ending. You slam on the brakes, but your car skids and swerves out of control. Everything seems to be moving in slow motion. Seconds later, you open your eyes and take a deep breath. You can't believe it. Your car is teetering on the edge of a cliff! If only you had stopped when you saw the sign! You utter God's name and what may be your last prayer. If only you had obeyed that sign.

In Matthew 7:15, Jesus warns, *"Watch out for false prophets. They come to you in sheep's clothing, but inwardly they are ferocious wolves."* How many proceed through life without heeding Christ's words of caution? How many pay little attention to the road signs of life, the signs God gives us to live life His way?

The number of souls perishing under the teachings of false preachers is truly staggering. Sometimes their lies are blatant; other times, they are more subtle. How do you recognize a false prophet? Matthew 7:16–20 clearly answers that question:

> *By their fruit you will recognize them. Do people pick grapes from thornbushes, or figs from thistles? Likewise every good tree bears good fruit, but a bad tree bears bad fruit. A good tree cannot bear bad fruit, and a bad tree cannot bear good fruit. Every tree that does not bear good fruit is cut down and thrown into the fire. Thus, by their fruit you will recognize them.*

At first glance, false prophets may not be obvious. Many present themselves very well in public. With smiles on their faces, they speak in tones that are polished and self-assured. But first impressions cannot always be trusted! To recognize a false prophet, one must carefully examine his life from the pulpit and the home. One must vigilantly dissect his message to the church using the most powerful Book at your disposal: the Bible. God assures us that we will be able to identify "bad trees." It is our spiritual responsibility to do so. What should you look for? Start by answering these two questions:

- Does the preacher's life match what he preaches?
- Is the preacher preaching the entire Word of God?

The first question may be difficult to answer. You can't follow a preacher around day and night or hide in a closet to see how he treats his spouse and kids. You can't barge into the church and hang around for weeks, watching how he interacts with the staff and members of the congregation. You can, however, meet with the pastor in order to get to know him better. You can observe his spirit, and you can pray for God to reveal the minister's true heart to you. Then you can make a wise decision about where you will attend church, and who will be guiding you and your family in your spiritual lives.

The second question can be answered only by Christians who actually *know* the Bible. Remember, it is your responsibility, not just the preacher's, to understand the Scriptures. Second Timothy 2:15 tells us, *"Do your best to present yourself to God as one approved, a workman who does not need to be ashamed and who correctly handles ("rightly dividing" NKJV) the word of truth."*

False prophets can be identified by the things they say and the things they do. If your pastor preaches unbiblical messages or participates in activities that you feel are unholy, it is your responsibility to talk with him first—not with other members of the congregation. Prayerfully and kindly talk with him about your concerns. James 5:19–20 reminds us of this truth:

> *My brothers, if one of you should wander from the truth and someone should bring him back, remember this: Whoever turns a sinner from the error of his way will save him from death and cover over a multitude of sins.*

Galatians 6:1 says, *"Brothers, if someone is caught in a sin, you who are spiritual should restore him gently. But watch yourself, or you also may be tempted."*

I can hear some say, "Wait a minute! You want me to go to my pastor and tell him he's in danger of becoming a false prophet?" The Scriptures clearly reveal we must confront people, no matter who they are, and show them the error of their ways; we must do it with meekness, humility, wisdom, and love. Remember that *"God shows no partiality"* (Acts 10:34 NKJV). Pastors need accountability as much as the members of the congregation need it. Spirit-filled people should hold one another accountable—always *"speaking the truth in love"* (Eph. 4:15). A further word of caution is needed here. "Fruit inspecting" can turn into self-righteous judging if the Holy Spirit is not in control of your life. Never judge another person without being willing to accept the same kind of judgment on your own life. (See Matthew 7:1–6.)

Second Peter 2:1 warns of the danger of listening to false teachings. It says that false prophets and teachers "will secretly introduce destructive heresies, even denying the sovereign Lord who bought them—bringing swift destruction on themselves." Here are five prominent lies being spread by false prophets of our day.

Lie #1: Walk down this aisle, and you will be saved. Where is this teaching in the Bible? It's not! Please don't misunderstand. If you are going forward to the altar in order to repent of your sins, renounce your former way of life, and give your heart to the Lord, then doing it in public is very biblical. As Luke 12:8–9 teaches,

> *Whoever acknowledges me before men, the Son of Man will also acknowledge him before the angels of God. But he who disowns me before men will be disowned before the angels of God.*

Too many preachers, though, are guilty of not emphasizing the need for repentance and a changed lifestyle through the indwelling of God's Spirit in the seeker's heart. Some preachers need to more fully emphasize these biblical truths as they invite people to the altar. Telling people that all they have to do to be saved is to walk down the church aisle, raise a hand, or sign a card gives people a false sense of security. Only Jesus can save lost sinners. Repentance and a subsequent reliance on Jesus Christ is what saves people from hell, not walking down a church aisle. As 1 John 1:9 clearly states, *"If we confess our sins, he is faithful and just and will forgive us our sins and purify us from all unrighteousness."*

Lie #2: God wants every Christian to be rich. Paul, who wrote much of the New Testament, had to support himself in part by his tentmaking skills. Although some churches sent him gifts at various times, he often provided for his own needs by the work of his hands. Yet Paul was rich—rich in the gifts of God. Money was not a priority in his life. In addition, many of the apostles in the early church renounced worldly wealth as an impediment to their relationship with the Lord.

God's blessings sometimes include money, but most of the time His blessings are spiritual in nature. He gives gifts, such as peace, joy, love, patience, and hope. God is more concerned with your character than the size of your house or bank account. Matthew 6:33 tells us where our focus should be: *"But seek first his kingdom and his righteousness, and all these things will be given to you as well."*

Be wary of preachers who spend more time talking about God's physical and monetary blessings than His spiritual blessings. Yes, God certainly is able to heal any sickness, but we don't serve Him for what He can do for us. It's also true that rich people can be saved; they can love and serve God in dynamic ways. Yet God knows that the temptations that come with wealth and prestige are often more than many can handle. Don't be fooled by handsome preachers in thousand-dollar suits who promise health and wealth in this world; instead, seek God and let Him decide how He wants to bless you.

Lie #3: God is love; therefore, it doesn't matter how I live. This half-truth gives a partial picture of the Lord—a picture that distorts the true character of God. The Bible says, *"God is love"* (1 John 4: 8, 16). He loves people—sinners and saints alike. He is *"not willing that any should perish, but that all should come to repentance"* (2 Peter 3:9 KJV). He loved us so much that He *"gave his one and only Son, that whoever believes in him shall not perish but have eternal life"* (John 3:16). Yet the way to heaven is *"narrow"* (Matt. 7:13), *"and only a few find it"* (v. 14).

The fruits of this feel-good doctrine—talking only about God's love and ignoring the need for repentance and obedience—can be seen in many churches. These church members become disillusioned when difficulties overwhelm them. They become angry and bitter when disciplined by God. They excuse their own sins and adopt the worldview that absolute right and wrong is narrow-minded and bigoted. The essential ingredients missing in this teaching are God's holiness, His divine standards, and His hatred of sin. Amos 5:15 says, *"Hate evil, love good."* God wants us to understand what He thinks about sin. God's love does not excuse us from our sins; instead, it demands justice for them. Only Jesus Christ can provide that justice in His shed blood at Calvary.

Lie #4: All the world's religions point to the same God. This devilish doctrine completely discounts the most fundamental truths in Scripture. Jesus Christ claimed to be equal with God Almighty. As He shared the Last Supper with His disciples, He told them,

> *"I am the way and the truth and the life. No one comes to the Father except through me. If you really knew me, you would know my Father as well. From now on, you do know him and have seen him." Philip said, "Lord, show us the Father and that will be enough for us." Jesus answered: "Don't you know me, Philip, even after I have been among you such a long time? Anyone who has seen me has seen the Father."* (John 14:6–9)

Wow! Jesus Christ is the unique God-man and the only One who can grant you citizenship into heaven. Many of the world's religions hold Jesus in high regard as a great teacher or prophet, but they refuse to believe that He is the Son of God. The only way I know to determine absolute truth is to go to the Source of it: Jesus Christ and the Bible that speaks of Him. If you believe the Bible, God's divine words and thoughts, then you won't believe the lies of false prophets and preachers who discount the deity of Jesus Christ.

Lie #5: God will always give us peace and safety. The devil has been spewing this lie for a long, long time. When sin overtakes us, the righteous anger of the Lord is aroused. Israel often fell into sin on a national level, and instead of repenting and seeking God, they turned their backs on Him and surrounded themselves with false prophets who told them what they wanted to hear. God spoke to the people through Jeremiah and said,

> *To whom can I speak and give warning? Who will listen to me? Their ears are closed so they cannot hear. The word of the LORD is offensive to them; they find no pleasure in it. But I am full of the wrath of the LORD, and I cannot hold it in. "Pour it out on the children in the street and on the young men gathered together; both husband and wife will be caught in it, and the old, those weighed down with years. Their houses will be turned over to others, together with their fields and their wives, when I stretch out my hand against those who live in the land," declares the LORD. "From the least to the greatest, all are greedy for gain; prophets and priests alike, all practice deceit. They dress the wound of my people as though it were not serious. 'Peace, peace,' they say, when there is no peace. Are they ashamed of their loathsome conduct? No, they have no shame at all; they do not even know how to blush. So they will fall among the fallen; they will be brought down when I punish them," says the LORD.*
> (Jer. 6:10–15)

Repeatedly, false prophets promised Israel peace and safety, but it was a peace and safety God couldn't deliver because they had rebelled against Him. God doesn't reward disobedience; on the contrary, He punishes it. Christians will experience peace in their hearts but will often experience war from the devil and the world because of their stand for God. Christians will experience safety from hell but will often experience trials and tribulations and disasters as they walk with the Lord. If you doubt this truth, carefully study the lives of the apostles. Most were brutally killed for their faith. God's ways are not always our ways. Don't rely on human reasoning; instead, allow the Lord to transform the way you think.

The pastor strolled and strutted across the church platform. He wore his million-dollar smile, designer suits, shiny cufflinks, and silk Italian ties proudly. His five-thousand-seat church was always filled every Sunday morning by people wanting to hear the "positive" side of the Gospel. His television and radio audiences reached millions; he shared that fact any chance he could.

As the church service ended, Pastor Park quickly exited through the back door behind the platform. He checked his watch.

"I'm going to be late again," he mumbled to himself as his Mercedes came into view.

Suddenly, a lady in her sixties appeared out of nowhere.

"Excuse me, Pastor Park."

The pastor, completely caught off guard, stopped. He wasn't used to people cornering him in the back parking lot. He bolted from the stage in order to prevent this kind of thing. He fixed what appeared to be a genuine smile on his face before asking, "Can I help you with something?"

Although his words were kind, the tone of his voice revealed that he didn't want to be bothered; he had more important things to do.

"Well, yes, you can, Pastor." She moved closer to him. "How do I get to heaven?"

The pastor stared at her for a long while before responding. "Why don't you make an appointment with one of my assistants? I'm sure they would be happy to help you on your spiritual journey."

"But, Pastor Park," continued the lady, undeterred by his lack of interest, "I really need your help."

The pastor glanced at his watch, then toward his car.

"Are you a member of my church?"

She quickly asked, "What does that have to do with anything?"

"Well," he began, his eyes darting around the parking lot, "I don't generally handle these matters. I have a wonderful staff who—"

She interrupted, "Pastor, please give me two minutes of your time." The look on her face grew serious. "It's a matter of life and death."

The pastor sighed. He didn't want to be responsible for the suicide of an elderly lady. It wouldn't look good in the newspapers.

He paused to choose the right words. "Are you contemplating...uh...taking your life?"

The lady appeared shocked by his question.

"No, I'm not. I just need to know how a person gets to heaven."

The pastor decided he would give her two—maybe three—minutes, max.

"I think it would pay you huge dividends to become a member of my church."

"You mean that will get me to heaven?"

"Well, it would be a good first step."

The lady studied him closely.

"Pastor, how do I get to heaven?"

Her repetition began to annoy him.

"You have to ask Jesus into your heart."

She nodded. "How will that get me to heaven?"

Pastor Park took a deep breath. He was trying to control his impatience.

"When you ask Him into your heart, He saves you and gives you eternal life."

She smiled. "So all I have to do is say a prayer, and I'm on my way to heaven?"

The pastor quickly nodded. "Yes, ma'am. Heaven is just a prayer away!"

Her face turned stern. "Tell me something, Pastor. Where does it say that in the Bible?" The lady's confrontational tone completely caught the pastor off guard.

"Ma'am, I don't want to get into a theological argument with you. There are thousands of ways to interpret the Bible, and I'm late for—"

She cut him off.

"How can I be sure I'm going to heaven?"

The lady's sincerity shook him to the core. In his fifteen years as a pastor, he had never had an encounter like this. He stepped to the side and slowly moved toward his car.

"You appear to be a godly person. I think your chances are quite high."

He picked up his stride, hoping she would disappear. She obviously didn't understand that he was a busy and important man. As he neared his gold sedan, with the license plate that read, "LUV-ALL," a rush of wind suddenly stormed from above. It knocked him flat on his back. Seconds later, he opened his eyes. Groggily, he stared toward heaven. His mouth dropped open at the sight. The elderly lady was rising into a vacuum of white clouds. Even from a distance, he could see tears streaming down her face as angelic wings sprouted from her sides. He moaned as he rubbed the large bump on the back of his head. As a gentle breeze glided over him, the Holy Spirit spoke to his soul. Her question kept ringing in his head. "How do I get to heaven?" For the first time in a long time, he wondered if he knew the answer.

This story depicts a spiritual cancer in our society today. Now, not everybody who wears expensive clothes is a compromiser or spiritual fraud; not every person who can afford a nice car is out of God's will. The pastor in this story is fictional and does not represent a specific individual, but his attitude and theology are rampant in many modern churches, both large and small.

What is God's attitude toward preachers who pervert His Word? Before reading further, would you take the time to read Jeremiah 23? Then let's look at several key thoughts contained in this powerful chapter.

In the first verse, Jeremiah addressed God's message to the religious leaders of the day: *"Woe to the shepherds who are destroying and scattering the sheep of my pasture!"* In contrast to Jesus, the *"good shepherd"* (John 10:11, 14), the preachers and religious teachers in Jeremiah's day were irresponsible, uncaring shepherds. They had provoked God by teaching *"visions from their own minds, not from the mouth of the LORD"* (v. 16).

God pronounced a curse on these Old Testament preachers for *"destroying and scattering the sheep."* His accusations against the false prophets were specific. He said they—

- *"follow an evil course and use their power unjustly"* (v. 10),
- *"led my people Israel astray"* (v. 13),
- *"commit adultery and live a lie"* (v. 14),
- *"strengthen the hands of evildoers"* (v. 14).

God wants His shepherds to feed His sheep, giving them the Word of God in a way that is understandable and helpful in living a godly life. He wants them to teach people to have a holy fear of God and not to be anxious about the things of this world. Knowing that God is in complete control frees believers from worries about this life. As Jesus said in Matthew 6:25, *"Do not worry about your life, what you will eat or drink; or about your body, what you will wear. Is not life more important than food, and the body more important than clothes?"* False prophets

seek followers who will trust in them, instead of relying entirely on God.

God's heart breaks as He sees false preachers masquerading as anointed ones. It arouses the righteous anger of the Lord to see smooth-tongued preachers replace the Word of God with cleverly invented ideas that contain only a shred of truth. Proverbs 14:12 reminds us that *"there is a way that seems right to a man, but in the end it leads to death."* Many discount the divine nature of the Word of God and reject its inerrancy. If a group of false prophets had to come to a consensus on the infallibility of the Bible, probably the only thing they would agree on would be the front and back covers!

Jesus told the false prophets of His day,

> *You belong to your father, the devil, and you want to carry out your father's desire. He was a murderer from the beginning, not holding to the truth, for there is no truth in him. When he lies, he speaks his native language, for he is a liar and the father of lies.*

False preachers do not *"correctly* [handle] *the word of truth"* (2 Tim. 2:15). They come up with their own interpretations to advance their own agendas. Their unregenerate hearts create their own versions of right and wrong, leading many astray. God warns those who follow them: *"They fill you with false hopes"* (Jer. 23:16), hopes that cannot save you from the fiery pit. They lead people into vanity. They teach beliefs systems that do not atone for sin. The lost in church flock to such preachers because they offer the hope of heaven without the sacrifices.

> *For such men are false apostles, deceitful workmen, masquerading as apostles of Christ. And no wonder, for Satan himself masquerades as an angel of light. It is not surprising, then, if his servants masquerade as servants of righteousness. Their end will be what their actions deserve.* (2 Cor. 11:13–15)

The lost in church are blinded to the truth in these verses. Many don't believe in a literal devil, which leads them to question right and wrong. Ethics become situational rather than moral. When you deny absolute truth, there is no longer a standard by which to measure good and evil.

Satan's master plan has always been to attack the church and not secular society. The devil already has control outside the church; that battle has already been won. Prophecy clearly states that the devil will employ a false prophet at the end of the age, a prophet who will lead much of the world astray to worship Satan instead of God. He will be working from inside the church to convert the religious (but not the saved) crowd to his brand of worship.

His battle plan is the same today! How many false preachers know they are working for the enemy? It's impossible to give a firm number, but I believe most don't know that they've sold out to the evil one and rejected the grace offered to them by the Lord. Satan's deception can be so convincing that, without God's help, *even the elect—if that were possible*" (Matt. 24:24) would be misled. Many false prophets today see themselves as Christians. They have been completely duped by the enemy and are now spreading their false doctrines to congregations around the world.

Johnny was sixteen years old with bright blue eyes and an even brighter intellect. When he was a toddler, his first word wasn't *Mama* or *Dada,* but *why*. His inquisitive nature had led him to the top of his junior class.

"America's War for Independence was a disaster for England," explained Mr. Riddle, Johnny's history teacher, as he wrote battle sites and dates on the blackboard.

Johnny's hand shot into the air as he said, "But, Mr. Riddle, I've been reading some books that suggest the war never occurred."

Mr. Riddle suddenly stopped writing. The chalk in his hand remained motionless as he slowly turned to face Johnny. He lowered his bifocals, staring at the student for what seemed like an eternity. Half the class watched the teacher; the other half kept their eyes on Johnny. Nobody said a word as the tension in the room mounted.

A grin spread over Mr. Riddle's face as he decided that Johnny was playing devil's advocate. "So you don't believe the Revolutionary War ever took place? Is that right?"

Johnny wasn't sure what to make of Mr. Riddle's amusement. "I'm just thinking outside the box," he said somewhat arrogantly.

"Outside the box?" the teacher questioned.

"Yeah, I mean...how do we really know it happened? Was anybody there that's alive today?"

The teacher couldn't believe his ears. Everybody knew Johnny was smart. His personality was somewhat cocky, but nobody expected him to challenge Mr. Riddle on something as basic as the Revolutionary War.

"Well," began the teacher, trying to defuse Johnny's pompous attitude, "you may have a valid point because, in reality, we can't prove you exist!"

The class burst into laughter. Johnny took their response personally.

"Maybe you should address the merit of my argument instead of insulting me."

The laugher quickly cooled. Mr. Riddle's bushy eyebrows slowly lifted toward his receding hairline.

"Okay, you want me to consider the merit of your argument?" his voice grew serious, making everyone, including Johnny, a little nervous. "You have no argument, Johnny. You're ignoring the facts. That's like saying two plus two no longer equals four. Or that the sun doesn't come up each morning and set every evening."

Johnny should have quit, but he didn't. He answered sarcastically, "It doesn't at the north pole in the winter."

Mr. Riddle's face turned red. He could not believe Johnny was acting like this in front of the whole class.

"Johnny, get serious. The facts are indisputable to anybody who's honest with them. Thousands of documents are still around today that detail every facet of this historic war." He waited for Johnny to respond.

Johnny's mind was spinning wildly. In a way, he had been joking. But now, seeing the response from his teacher, he wasn't about to stop.

"Isn't it possible for all those documents to be frauds, a cleverly disguised attempt to create a war for the express purpose of bolstering national pride?"

"How about similar documents from the British?" Mr. Riddle countered.

With a straight face, Johnny answered, "Frauds."

"How about the French?"

"The same."

Mr. Riddle knew that Johnny was too embarrassed to back down now. His arguments were becoming more outrageous. Mr. Riddle decided to put an end to it.

"I think this has gone far enough, Johnny. Why don't you take up your ideas with a higher authority?" Mr. Riddle pulled out a notepad and scribbled something on it. "Here's a personal invitation to the principal's office."

The smile on Johnny's face disappeared.

False prophets discount the authority of the Bible. They will argue in circles, using half-truths in an effort to "support" their positions. But truth does not change. In spite of what false teachers may say, the truths of Jesus Christ do not shift with changing cultures or the rise and fall of governments. Jesus is one with the Father. God raised Him from the dead, and He is sitting at the right hand of God Almighty. Only Jesus can save people from their sins and give the gift of eternal life. Absolute truth comes from one place: the Bible. If you need law work, go to a lawyer. If you need medical attention, see a doctor. If you need your financial books done, visit an accountant.

And if you need the answers to life, go to the Author of Life, Jesus Christ.

Who are you trusting in? Your pastor? Your church? Your denomination? This is spiritual idolatry, and it is dangerous. God wants you to trust in His Son, Jesus Christ, and His Word, the Bible. He wants you to be part of His church in a place where you can grow in faith, serve in compassion, and love in word and deed.

> *But blessed is the man who trusts in the LORD, whose confidence is in him. He will be like a tree planted by the water that sends out its roots by the stream. It does not fear when heat comes; its leaves are always green. It has no worries in a year of drought and never fails to bear fruit.* (Jer. 17:7–8)

Chapter Ten

United in Love

*"By this all will know that you are My disciples,
if you have love for one another."*
—John 13:35 NKJV

If you want to see the true character of people, look at their home life. It is unlikely that you will get an accurate assessment just by observing someone at church, work, or in a social setting. The true character of an individual is revealed at home—seeing how the person interacts with his or her spouse, kids, and even the family pet. For most of us, it's not too difficult to put on our best faces for a couple of hours a day. But, at home, we let our guard down and reveal who we really are. When the makeup and masks come off, what does your family see? What do you see? What does God see?

Many lost in church struggle with interpersonal relationships—especially among those who know them best: their family. Your family knows what makes you tick—and what ticks you off. They know your weaknesses, sore spots, and fears. And your family knows when your walk does not match your talk.

Too many families are dysfunctional today. Could it be that many of them are among the lost in church? If so, they are unable to tap into the divine power that enables them to love and forgive unconditionally, and to stick it out when the pressures of life bear down upon them.

The air was thick with accusations and distrust. Twenty minutes with a marital counselor had only fanned the flames of anger between Rob and Cindy. Married for six years, they both worked full-time jobs, had two young children, and, for the most part, faithfully attended their local church.

Andy Pillar, a trained Christian counselor for nearly twenty years, had seen it all. *Struggling marriages like Rob and Cindy's are becoming more common than the measles,* he thought sadly. Although they were a good-looking couple, well thought of by neighbors, co-workers, and church members, their marriage was falling apart.

Cindy complained, "He doesn't listen to anything I say. He's more concerned with work and his buddies than with me!"

Rob immediately interjected, "That's not true! It's like she wants me to be her everything. She doesn't like it when I do anything but spend time with her and the kids."

"That's a lie!" she exclaimed. "I just want some respect!"

Rob slumped back in his seat and rolled his eyes. He was tired of fighting. When they were first married, it was easier to be the man he knew he should be, but things were different now. He was sick of the pain, the fighting, the disappointment. He zoned out as he dreamed about going away and escaping Cindy's constant nagging.

"Rob, are you with us?" asked Andy, waiting for Rob to respond.

Rob slowly returned his focus to the counselor. "I'm sorry. What did you say?"

Cindy interrupted. "You see! He's doing it here, too!"

Rob gave Cindy an angry look.

The counselor tried to contain the storm that was brewing. He spoke firmly but gently.

"Calm down, guys. Our purpose here is to strengthen your marriage—not attack one another. Now, Rob, why do you seem to zone out when Cindy is talking?"

Rob swallowed hard as he stared in Cindy's direction. He felt cornered. He wasn't used to examining his feelings, but he answered with the first thought that came to him.

"Well, she's not always the most pleasant person to be around."

Cindy's heart wilted at his words. She could tell that he wasn't deliberately trying to hurt her, yet hearing his words wasn't easy, especially when she knew there was a lot of truth in them.

The counselor looked at Cindy. "Cindy, when Rob hurts your feelings, what do you do with that hurt?"

The question confused Cindy. She had grown up in a family where constant feuding was the norm. Although she had dreamed of a loving marriage, she now wondered if they really existed. To her, marriage was mostly a commitment. Love was for dating—and for the birds.

She stammered to find the right words. "Well, I guess I just hope the hurt will go away." She shrugged her shoulders. "Give it enough time, and it'll be forgotten."

Andy scribbled something on his notepad, then turned toward Rob.

"What do you do with all the hurt you feel?"

Rob was ready for the question.

"That's when I zone out. I figure if I'm not emotionally connected to all this junk, I won't be hurt."

Andy nodded as he wrote down a couple words, underlining them twice. He breathed a prayer that Cindy and Rob would be receptive to what he was about to say.

"Well, we've been meeting for a couple of months now, and I've been listening to your concerns and hurts. I'm sure you would both agree that each of you needs to improve in certain areas before your marriage can return to its original purpose."

Cindy forced a smile; Rob tried to hide an embarrassed smirk. Andy watched the couple for a moment, observing their non-verbal communication. They had grown used to blaming each other for the failure of their marriage.

"I asked you two what you did with all the hurt, with all the sins that you have committed against each other and the Lord. Your answers have really helped me to understand how I, and more important, how the Lord can help you fall in love with each other again."

Cindy looked at Rob as if to say, "You'd better be listening."

"I'm going to ask each of you a deeply personal question. Do I have your permission?"

Cindy nodded and nervously smiled; Rob nodded and winced.

"When did you become born again?"

Neither said a word as the counselor waited for their answers. He was silently praying for God to transform their lives and their marriage. Cindy spoke first.

"I was seventeen years old. It happened at a summer youth camp."

Andy asked, "Are you completely sure it was a real salvation experience?"

Cindy didn't hesitate with her reply.

"Absolutely. The troubles didn't seem to start until several years into the marriage."

"What troubles are you talking about?"

A single tear ran down her face.

"I know I'm out of God's will. I mean, I know I'm backslidden." She reached for a tissue. Andy noticed a hint of compassion in Rob's expression. Cindy broke down. "I just don't know what to do about it. Every time I try to do the right thing, I fail...miserably."

Rob reached for her hand. He hadn't seen this kind of humility from Cindy in eons.

"Cindy," began the counselor, "you've allowed bitterness to take control of your life. You've given the devil a foothold, and you're trying to hold him back with your own will and power." Andy edged forward in his seat.

"You will always lose that fight if you try to do it on your own. You've got to use God's power to break the evil that's dominating you."

Rob slowly caressed her clammy hand. She looked at her husband and sobbed, "Am I really such a bad wife?"

Rob didn't know what to say. He glanced at Andy for direction.

Andy said, "It's not about being a bad wife. It's about listening to God instead of Satan. Don't concentrate on how bad or good you've been; concentrate on what God wants to do in your life today."

His words helped to calm her.

"Okay," she said softly.

"What do you think God wants from you today?" the counselor asked.

She looked at Rob through her tears.

"He wants me to love my husband no matter..." Her voice trailed off. Then she smiled as she said, "No matter how much of a jerk he is."

Rob laughed, which relieved Andy.

"I've been a jerk once or twice in my life," Rob admitted.

Andy continued. "So what are you going to do with all your hurt and anger, Cindy?"

"I need to give it to the Lord." Suddenly, she realized that she had known the answer all along. It was simple enough for a child to understand, yet she had dismissed it out of pride.

"And what about the next time you and Rob have a disagreement?"

Cindy knew the answer.

"I've got to live one day at a time and constantly ask for God's help to love my husband and to be the person the Lord wants me to be."

As they prayed, Cindy felt the weight of her sin lifting. The Holy Spirit was cleansing her and opening her heart to the truths that had eluded her during her years of marriage.

"How do you feel?" Andy asked, seeing the light in her eyes return.

"Stupid." She smiled. "Stupid for letting all this stuff eat me alive and not turning to God in the first place."

Andy nodded and then looked at Rob.

"Your turn."

Rob's joy quickly turned to gloom.

"What?"

Andy glanced at his notes.

"You said that you often run from problems, hoping they'll go away."

"I'm not sure I said I run from problems."

The counselor smiled and asked, "When did you get saved, Rob?"

His response was almost mechanical. "I was ten years old."

Andy waited for more information but didn't get it.

"Can you tell me more about what happened?"

Rob hesitated. "Ah...well...I don't really remember the details, but I'm sure I asked Jesus into my heart."

Cindy stared at her husband with compassion instead of hatred. She had never talked with him about his relationship with the Lord. She had just assumed he was a Christian because he went to church.

"Why are you sure?"

"Are you saying I'm not a Christian?" Rob asked defensively.

Andy didn't break eye contact with him. He had seen this reaction many times before.

"It doesn't matter what I think. This is between you and God."

Rob looked down, embarrassed by his outburst. There was a long, awkward silence. Rob didn't have the courage to proceed, but Andy wisely remained silent. Cindy started to say something, but Andy quickly shook his head. God was working, and he didn't want anybody getting in the way.

Rob softly uttered, "I guess I'm not really sure if I was saved. I remember saying the prayer of salvation with the youth pastor, but it all seems like a hazy memory now."

Andy's response was gentle.

"Was there a change in your behavior?"

"Nah...not really. I got into my share of trouble as a teenager."

"Do you think salvation leads to a changed lifestyle?"

Rob shrugged. Deep down in his heart, he knew the answer, but he wasn't eager to admit it.

"I guess."

"If you don't remember a change in your life, in your attitudes, your habits, your actions, then that's a pretty good sign that your conversion wasn't genuine."

Cindy sat motionless. She couldn't believe what she was hearing, though it did explain Rob's lack of interest in praying with her and the kids, his lack of desire to read the Bible, and his refusal to attend church more than on Sunday mornings.

Rob wanted to get out of there. He felt like telling the counselor to mind his own business—to just leave him alone. He wanted to run, but he didn't.

When he finally spoke, his sincerity was obvious. "Maybe I'm backslidden." Rob glanced at Cindy. She squeezed his hand in support.

"Rob," Andy said lovingly, "only God knows if you're backslidden or if you've never been saved. I've found that most people know themselves deep down. To have the Holy Spirit in your life—the most powerful force in the universe—and not know it is quite unlikely."

Rob dropped his head. Something inside him, something unfamiliar yet inviting, was telling him to give up the fight—to admit his need for God. Cindy and Andy sensed the presence of the Holy Spirit and closed their eyes in prayer. Tears trickled down Rob's cheeks as the last wall separating him from God crashed down. He had been fooling himself for so long. Christianity had become a habit, a ritual, something he did because he had always done it. He knew the truth but had rejected it. He knew the way but didn't want to give up his pleasures, his sins—or the control. He knew what God expected of him. Before, it had scared him, but now, he was prepared to do it. The pain, deception, and loneliness he had been living with were more than he could take. Rob always knew he needed Christ, but now...he wanted Christ.

"I'm ready," he announced boldly.

The counselor smiled as he reached his hand across the desk.

"Let's all three hold hands as we talk to the Father."

Cindy was smiling from ear to ear as she closed her eyes. She knew this was the start of a whole new life—a life in which they would both be dedicated to God. She knew it wouldn't be easy and that all their problems wouldn't suddenly go away. Yet she also realized that they would have a powerful new force on their side to help them deal with anything that came their way.

No matter how strong your walk with the Lord is, marriage relationships will have their problems—times when one or both partners give in to sin or selfishness. This fictional story was not created to send a message that born-again Christians won't have problems, or that they won't need counseling or therapy at times. Instead, it was written to reveal the satanic deception prevalent in many households today. Family problems can be solved when the members within the family are saved. Personal habits that destroy relationships can be overcome by the power of God. Failing marriages can be repaired if partners give up their backslidden ways and turn wholeheartedly to the Savior.

Our God is the same God who performed miracles in the Bible. God wants to perform a miracle in your family. Do you believe He can?

I'll never forget the day my wife Tina and I were in a premarital counseling session. At our last meeting, the pastor had given us a list of questions to be filled out and returned. Here's the story as I remember it.

"You two have those questions I gave you?" asked Pastor Brooks, a young man in his mid-thirties.

I smiled as I yanked them from the back pocket of my jeans.

"Right here," I said, handing them across the desk.

"And you filled these out together?" the pastor asked.

Tina and I looked at each other and smiled. "Yes," we said together.

I grabbed Tina's hand and looked lovingly into her eyes. Young love was new, exciting, and so very promising. I thought, *Nothing is ever going to rob me of this feeling.*

Within seconds of reading our answers, the pastor started laughing. In fact, he nearly fell off his seat. We weren't sure if we should laugh with him or be upset.

He said, "I'm sorry, guys. It's just that you seem to have these answers down to a tee." He pointed to question number five. "It's this one that really got to me."

I grabbed the paper as Tina looked on. It read, "What do you plan on doing when you and your spouse get into a heated argument?" We had written, "We will get on our knees together, hold hands, and pray that God will restore our love for one another."

I looked at Pastor Brooks and said, "I don't get it. I thought that was the right answer."

Quickly, he assured us, "Yes, you're right. It's just that I've never been too successful in doing it. But if you two can, then more power to you."

I glanced at my future wife thinking, Wow, this guy's not as spiritual as I thought.

Years later, I understand why he was laughing. He couldn't help but be amused by our idealism. I don't have a perfect marriage, nor do I think one actually exists. In the heat of the moment, I've learned that Christianity is often forgotten as the flesh tries to overbear the

Spirit within. No matter how close your walk is with the Lord, you will stumble, you will fall, and you will make a fool of yourself. The difference between the lost in church and the true church is simple: The lost consistently fall from grace and don't repent; the saved fall less often and when they do, they seek God's and each other's forgiveness.

In addition to not having the Spirit to help them with their relationships, the lost in church have misplaced values. They may know the priorities that God has set for mankind, but few actually put that knowledge into action. And remember, saving faith requires us to act on the knowledge we have—not just give it lip service. This list of priorities based on scriptural principles will help to create a God-centered marriage.

God
Spouse
Kids
Job
Friends
Self

Many church families today are dysfunctional because of mixed-up priorities. Their list may look something like this:

Job
Self
Kids
Spouse
God
Friends

No matter how you look at things, Jesus Christ must come first in your marriage and family relationships. There's nothing more important than centering your life and your family on God. Remember, He is a jealous God, and He will take steps, sometimes painful steps, to bring you in line with His desires. Your life will never function properly when you are out of His will. So if things aren't going the way you like, carefully examine your priorities. Realize that God may be trying to get your attention. He loves you too much to allow you to foul up in this critical area.

The second priority in your Christian walk must be your spouse. Genesis 2:24 says, "For this reason a man will leave his father and mother and be united to his wife, and they will become one flesh." Ephesians 5:28–30 states,

> *In this same way, husbands ought to love their wives as their own bodies. He who loves his wife loves himself. After all, no one ever hated his own body, but he feeds and cares for it, just as Christ does the church—for we are members of his body.*

You are spiritually joined with your spouse. Scripture likens the earthly love between a husband and a wife to the love Jesus has for His bride, the church.

It is critical that you place your spouse above your job, friends, and yes, even your children. This doesn't mean you don't take care of your kids or that you show them less love. Nor do you neglect their emotional needs. On the contrary, it means you show your spouse the love he or she deserves so your kids can grow up learning what true love means. Try to plan time with each other at least once a week if possible in order to nurture your relationship. Your kids will benefit from the security of having parents who love each other.

Part of the Christian life is putting others before yourself. Your children are not only gifts from God; they are your responsibility. Of course, parents must provide the necessities like shelter, food, and clothing. But they must also give their children tenderness, compassion, time, and a Christian witness—in a word, love. Too many parents, especially fathers, provide financially for their families without providing the emotional and spiritual support that creates a healthy, happy home. Those who are lost in church are often negligent in this matter as they try to keep up with the Joneses. Money and possessions can never be a substitute for your time and love. I've never seen a mansion give a kid a hug or an expensive toy cheer him on at a sporting event or a vacation repair the damage from a year of neglect. Are we going to teach children the value of love or the value of money?

Of course, we must work to provide the necessities of life. It's part of the original curse from Adam's and Eve's rebellion. Genesis 3:17–19 says,

> *Cursed is the ground because of you; through painful toil you will eat of it all the days of your life. It will produce thorns and thistles for you, and you will eat the plants of the field. By the sweat of your brow you will eat your food until you return to the ground, since from it you were taken; for dust you are and to dust you will return.*

Although your job falls near the bottom of the totem pole, it often takes you from your family for a portion of each day. For some reading this book, God is calling you to a new job or career, an occupation that will give you more time with your family. For others, He's calling you to stay home with your children and to raise them in the knowledge of the Lord. There are still others to whom the Holy Spirit is speaking, telling you to slow down, cut back, and take time to get to know your family again. Whatever your situation, the Holy Spirit will speak to you. Spend time seeking God's guidance, and He will give you the answer that is best for your family.

You may have noticed that I prioritized friends before self. Your circle of friends and acquaintances should be a fantastic place to show your Christian witness. They need to see the godly priorities in your life and your vibrant personal walk with God. They need to know that you keep your word and that you will stick with them through thick and thin. Your influence can make a difference in someone's living a life of purity or compromise. Even more significantly, you can make a difference in someone's going to heaven or hell. Friends can also be an excellent source of encouragement for you during the dark trials of life. As Proverbs 17:17 says, *"A friend loves at all times, and a brother is born for adversity."*

We've come to the last word on the list: *You!* Does this make you less important than everybody else? Of course not! Does it mean you don't need to take care of yourself? No! Scripture clearly speaks to this issue. Here are only a few verses that help us understand how we should view ourselves.

Jesus said, *"If anyone would come after me, he must deny himself and take up his cross and follow me"* (Matt. 16:24). We must give up what we want and do what God wants. We must leave behind our sinful ways and follow Him in righteousness. Giving up our desires places God in the captain's seat of our lives. Who do you think is more qualified to fill that position, you or Jesus?

Philippians 2:3–4 says, "Do nothing out of selfish ambition or vain conceit, but in humility consider others better than yourselves. Each of you should look not only to your own interests, but also to the interests of others." Jesus wants His people to give to others, to have an attitude of humility instead of pride. He wants the church to act more like a family rather than a business where it's "every man for himself."

What does Scripture say about being a godly wife or husband? Before we delve into these verses, let's make one thing clear: You cannot be the man or woman God desires you to be without a relationship with Him. The Holy Spirit must be in full control of your life. Can you imagine a pilot having partial control of his aircraft?

Would you want to fly in those unfriendly skies? Would you take one step onto that aircraft? Ask any trained pilot what would happen if he lost an engine or the stabilizers or the rudder. Likewise, giving God partial control of your life is a recipe for disaster. He wants all of you. The lost in church try valiantly to succeed with their families, yet most fail miserably. They fail because they are trusting in man-made techniques rather than God's. Here's a short list of man's remedies to enhance your marriage and family life. None of these have *lasting* success.

- Secular books touting secrets to a happy family
- Drugs and herbs to promote well-being
- Modern psychology that ignores man's sinfulness and his need for a Savior
- Mandatory church attendance for the kids while the parents stay home to do their own thing
- Giving kids more freedom and less discipline in the hopes of winning them over as your best friends
- Buying your spouse or kids more of what they want
- Trying really hard in your own strength, without asking God for help

This list could go on and on, but the main point is this: Is God at the center of your family? Is He the foundation of your marriage? Learn the Bible, study it diligently, and feed on it. God will give you wisdom. No matter where you are in your walk with God, He will guide you if You ask Him for His help. James 1:5 says, *"If any of you lacks wisdom, he should ask God, who gives generously to all without finding fault, and it will be given to him."*

Most reading this book have read the Scriptures dealing with husbands and wives. (See, for example, Ephesians 5:21–30 and Colossians 3:18–21.) Instead of focusing on those popular verses about marriage, let's look at the qualifications for a man to be an elder, bishop, or deacon. These verses describe what it means to be a godly man; they aptly apply to God's expectations for men as fathers and husbands.

> *Now the overseer must be above reproach, the husband of but one wife, temperate, self-controlled, respectable, hospitable, able to teach, not given to drunkenness, not violent but gentle, not quarrelsome, not a lover of money. He must manage his own family well and see that his children obey him with proper respect. (If any-one does not know how to manage his own family, how can he take care of God's church?)...Deacons, likewise, are to be men worthy of respect, sincere, not indulging in much wine, and not pursuing dishonest gain. They must keep hold of the deep truths of the faith with a clear conscience.* (1 Tim. 3:2–5, 8–9)

Men, are you thinking these expectations are just a little more than you can handle? Do you feel like you did back in high school on the first day of French class? Remember when your teacher started speaking French fluently, and then smiled and told you that you would be doing the same thing by the end of the year? You wanted to drop out then and there. Yet through hard work and perseverance, you remained vigilant through the year. When June came, the words flowed effortlessly—well, almost effortlessly—from your lips.

Take heart! You don't have to accomplish all this instantaneously. Just as a child goes to school day after day, week after week, and year after year to acquire the knowledge necessary to live a productive life, so every man must go to God day after day, week after week, year after year to obtain the power and desire to be a godly husband and father. If you faithfully seek Him with all your heart, He will help you to become the man you can be.

This passage from 1 Timothy 3 calls for men to be *"above reproach"* (v. 2). The King James Version uses the word *"blameless."* God wants men to admit their

191

shortcomings instead of concealing them, to be led by the Spirit at every moment, and to repair any damaged family relationships through humility, repentance, and prayer. God wants men to live at peace. His Word says, *"Pursue peace with all people, and holiness, without which no one will see the Lord"* (Heb. 12:14 NKJV). A blameless man will pursue peace, especially with his family.

God desires men to be emotionally balanced in their family relationships—to be *"temperate, self-controlled"* (1 Tim. 3:2). Godly men do not live lives of extremes—one minute being angry and the next completely calm. They live on an even keel, like rocks in the midst of life's storms. They are a refuge for their families and provide courage, strength, and support. They seldom stray from the straight and narrow path; they keep their ship and its passengers safe as they maneuver through the rocky shoals of life.

They are also *"able to teach"* (v. 2). God wants men to be the spiritual leaders in their families. Their first course of action is to live and teach by example. They must practice what they preach and do what they say they're going to do. If they fail this basic test of leadership, the entire family structure will implode, leaving chaos and emotional wounds. Jesus Christ must be their Teacher. They must daily feed on spiritual truths from the Word of God.

If you ask the average Christian woman what she wants most in her husband, she will tell you she wants a husband who loves the Lord and shows it by loving his family unconditionally. Remember, men, you will teach your family more about God by what you do at home than by all the other activities you are involved in—no matter how religious they are.

Deuteronomy 11 reminds us,

Fix these words of mine in your hearts and minds; tie them as symbols on your hands and bind them on your

foreheads. Teach them to your children, talking about them when you sit at home and when you walk along the road, when you lie down and when you get up.
(Deut. 11:18–19)

No matter what time of day it is, God wants men to be teaching their families about God. Morning, noon, and night—day in, day out—at home or away, in the car or on the couch, we are to be teaching God's ways. For the Christian, vacation or retirement from the faith is not an option.

First Timothy 3 also calls for men not to be *"violent but gentle"* (v. 3). The gentle, loving hands of a godly man can do more healing than a roomful of doctors. Families need to experience God's love through their husbands and fathers. God wants men to be compassionate, able to place themselves in another's shoes, and willing to walk the extra mile whenever the need arises.

Jesus Christ is the gentle Lamb of God who calls people to *"be patient, bearing with one another in love"* (Eph. 4:2). Godly men need to practice this trait of our Lord; in return, God blesses their families with stability and peace in spite of life's changing circumstances.

Men filled with the Holy Spirit know how to handle family fights. They know how to confront issues fairly. They know how to defuse family situations before they blow up, and they know when to raise the white flag when surrender is necessary. Fighting and quarrels will happen in families; it's a matter of how you fight and in what spirit you fight.

I remember talking to a couple years ago. I asked them how often they fought. The husband proudly told me that they never fought. Never? Boy, was I impressed! I wondered what I was doing wrong. I thought maybe I wasn't being the proper Christian husband or maybe my wife wasn't being the proper Christian wife. What a shock I received the following year when I heard that this "perfect" couple was getting a divorce! I found out that they seldom communicated, and when they did, one demanded his or her way while the other hid in a self-imposed shell of pity and anger. No, they didn't fight in the traditional sense. Their war was hidden in their emotional bunkers of the heart. When the real shooting began, the marriage quickly vaporized into a string of skirmishes that ended with both sides losing.

A godly man is *"sincere"* (1 Tim. 3:8) or as the *New King James Version* states it, *"not double-tongued."* He speaks truth, not lies; compliments, not insults. A man's words are often a barometer of his spiritual condition. Proverbs 10:19–21 says,

> *When words are many, sin is not absent, but he who holds his tongue is wise. The tongue of the righteous is choice silver, but the heart of the wicked is of little value. The lips of the righteous nourish many, but fools die for lack of judgment.*

God wants men to speak in a measured way and use words wisely. I'm not saying that husbands should limit how much they talk to their families. Rather, they should think before they speak and pray for God's Spirit to be evident in their conversations. In the heat of the moment, don't give in to the lusts of the flesh and say something you will later regret. A man whose heart is intimately connected to God will have words like fresh water, words that feed and nourish the ears and hearts of those who hear him speak. This kind of family man will help his family grow spiritually, bringing them into a closer walk with God.

Men, a godly husband is not perfect, but he tries to be. Many men lost in church today are inadvertently leading their families down the same thorn-infested path they are following. God will hold the man responsible for leading his family astray. Men, the buck stops with you!

Okay, ladies. I could hear the loud "Amens" coming from your corner as you read what men should be like.

Well, it's your turn! Please don't put down the book or skip this part. Instead, ask God to speak to you as we look at the familiar passage from Proverbs 31. I know what you're thinking: "There's no way I could ever be like that woman! The expectations are way beyond my abilities." You're absolutely right—if you try to do it in your own strength. On the other hand, if you follow God's way and rely on His power, all things are possible. Remember, Jesus turned water into wine. He healed the sick, raised the dead, and came back to life. If you say, I can't, you may really be thinking, God can't. When you become more of the woman that God expects you to be, you make it easier for your man to do the same. Often, it's your godly example that can sharpen his faith, as well as that of your children's.

Who can find a virtuous wife? For her worth is far above rubies. The heart of her husband safely trusts her; so he will have no lack of gain. She does him good and not evil all the days of her life. She seeks wool and flax, and willingly works with her hands. She is like the merchant ships, she brings her food from afar. She also rises while it is yet night, and provides food for her household, and a portion for her maidservants. She considers a field and buys it; from her profits she plants a vineyard. She girds herself with strength, and strengthens her arms. She perceives that her merchandise is good, and her lamp does not go out by night. She stretches out her hands to the distaff, and her hand holds the spindle. She extends her hand to the poor, yes, she reaches out her hands to the needy. She is not afraid of snow for her household, for all her household is clothed with scarlet. She makes tapestry for herself; her clothing is fine linen and purple. Her husband is known in the gates, when he sits among the elders of the land. She makes linen garments and sells them, and supplies sashes for the merchants. Strength and honor are her clothing; she shall rejoice in time to come. She opens her mouth with wisdom, and on her tongue is the law of kindness. She watches over the ways of her household, and does not eat the bread of idleness. Her children rise up and call her blessed; her husband also, and he praises her: "Many daughters have done well, but you excel them all." Charm is deceitful and beauty is passing, but a woman who fears the LORD, she shall be praised. (Prov. 31:10–30 NKJV)

Did that description of a *"wife of noble character"* (v. 10 NIV) discourage you? Are you ready to forget you ever picked up this book? Hold on. Instead of focusing on all the duties this woman performed so well, let's look at several key characteristics from her life that will help you to become a more godly woman. Do you want to be a godly woman? If you really want that blessing, God will reward that spirit of faith.

Verse 11 says, *"Her husband has full confidence in her and lacks nothing of value."* Does your husband confide his deepest secrets to you? Does he have confidence that you will not betray him? Many woman lost in church try to manipulate their husbands by using sex, their kids, threats, or various other emotionally packed issues. Instead of seeking God's ways, they devise schemes, games, and guilt trips designed to bring their men into submission. This pattern of control places families on the superhighway to divorce. God wants a woman to possess His character and to be controlled by the Holy Spirit. A man finds "safety" in this kind of woman. He can turn to her instead of other women, drugs, alcohol, or any other worldly enticement. She satisfies his every need— from the spiritual to the emotional to the physical. When you become this godly person, you will own your husband's eyes and heart.

Verse 12 says, *"She brings him good, not harm, all the days of her life."* If a woman's heart is sold out to the Lord, she will create a pleasant atmosphere for her husband and kids. She will please the Lord by seeing after her husband's welfare and interests. When he reads

James 1:17, *"Every good and perfect gift is from above, coming down from the Father of the heavenly lights, who does not change like shifting shadows,"* he will smile and think of her.

Her friends, relatives, and her own interests will be secondary to her husband. If there is chaos at home, no manner of success outside the home will satisfy the longings of her soul. A woman must overcome her natural instinct to control her husband; however, that tendency can be destroyed only by the free-flowing power of the Holy Spirit in her life. Satan is crouching at the door of a woman's heart, hoping to entice her into this seductive but destructive behavior. Flee from the devil and his ways, and run into the waiting arms of your Lord. He is your hope, your joy and peace, your strength, and your salvation.

The first part of verse 25 states that *"she is clothed with strength and dignity."* A godly man longs for a woman who is strong in the Lord. The strength of a woman can be seen in her character, a measure of her faith in God. A woman with godly strength has the spiritual muscle to weather the storms of life without turning to worldly strategies that simply don't work.

A woman who loves God and shows it through her family life should be honored as much as writers, inventors, CEOs, or anybody else who accomplishes extraordinary tasks. Even if you never receive man's honor, the Creator of man, Jesus Christ, honors godly women. Ladies, take joy in knowing that Jesus is proud of you and blesses you when you obey Him. Galatians 6:9 should motivate you to continue your good works. *"And let us not grow weary while doing good, for in due season we shall reap if we do not lose heart"* (NKJV). Ladies, a day is coming when your love, hard work, and perseverance will pay off in ways you cannot fathom. People may not give you recognition now, but God will reward your dedication when you enter heaven.

Verse 25 also states, *"She can laugh at the days to come."* God desires that you would have no fear of the future—the future of your children, parents, husband, or anyone else close to you. The women lost in church are often consumed with worry and doubts, whereas the redeemed can literally be joyful and laugh at the future knowing that God is in control of their lives. Jesus addressed this issue with the people of His day:

> *So do not worry, saying, "What shall we eat?" or "What shall we drink?" or "What shall we wear?" For the pagans run after all these things, and your heavenly Father knows that you need them. But seek first his kingdom and his righteousness, and all these things will be given to you as well.* (Matt. 6:31–33)

Even godly women can fall for the enemy's traps: worrying about finances, kids, husbands, and a host of other issues that aren't that significant in the bigger picture of life. Do you trust God with your future? Do you believe He's in total control of your life? Give Jesus full reign in your life, and you won't have to worry. He knows what's best for you. His Word says, *"If you, then, though you are evil, know how to give good gifts to your children, how much more will your Father in heaven give good gifts to those who ask him!"* (Matt. 7:11).

Verse 26 says, *"She speaks with wisdom, and faithful instruction is on her tongue."* A wise woman is a precious jewel, her worth far greater than any worldly gem. God desires a Christian woman to have His mind, to possess a knowledge of heavenly truths that can transform an ordinary lady into a miracle of generosity and kindness.

Notice the Scripture doesn't just say she has wisdom, but that *"faithful instruction is on her tongue."* God's Holy Spirit flows through her like a river of water carving through a barren landscape. That river can drastically alter, mold, and form the surrounding countryside. Have you ever seen a river flowing through a desert? Trees and tropical vegetation flower against the backdrop of the barren landscape. In a world filled with death, you can be that light, that life, that stands out in the crowd. Likewise, a wise woman can alter, mold, and form her family's, friends', and coworkers' perceptions and beliefs of God. A wise woman can hold her tongue when she senses bitterness or anger in her spirit. She can resist lashing out when others have hurt her and leave judgment to the Lord. Ladies, invest your time, energy, and talents into finding wisdom, for when you do, you are literally seeking the mind of God.

Many lost in church today scoff at the old-fashioned religion of their grandparents, considering their beliefs to be narrow-minded and outdated. But, I ask you, are we in the church happier today than our ancestors were? Oh yes, we have our modern conveniences and comfortable lifestyles, but do we have peace, joy, and the Lord's blessing on our families?

The thread holding the fabric of our nations together is the family. In country after country and city after city, the seams are unraveling at a dizzying pace. As the divorce rate climbs, sexual promiscuity skyrockets, and selfish ambitions increase, the Lord is still looking for godly men and women who will be united in love to one another, to their children, and to Him. One standing alone can be easily overtaken. Two joined together gain strength in their unity, but three combined are formidable. As Ecclesiastes 4:12 says, *"A cord of three strands is not quickly broken."* Jesus wants to join you and your spouse in a cord of love that is impenetrable. Jesus can transform your family into a testimony of His love and grace. What's stopping Him in your life?

Chapter Eleven

Proudhearted or Poor in Spirit?

"When pride comes, then comes disgrace,
but with humility comes wisdom."
—Proverbs 11:2

S atan has at his disposal weapons of mass destruction. His instruments are more deadly than present-day biological, chemical, or nuclear armaments. His most lethal weapon has destroyed countless numbers of people over the course of history. It doesn't contain a rocket, a canister, bullets, fuel, or powder. Consequently, many do not recognize its destructive power. Some even see it as admirable, unaware of the damage it can inflict.

I'm speaking of religious pride. This type of pride is subtle, yet it is capable of destroying soul and spirit. Religious pride can affect anyone at any time, and it is one of the chief weapons Satan uses against the lost in church.

Pastor Evan Billings was not looking forward to this meeting, yet he knew the Holy Spirit had called for it. Dean Walters had been a deacon in the church for more than thirty years, twenty-five years longer than Pastor Billings had served there. As the young pastor sat at his desk reviewing his notes for the meeting, the knot in his tie seemed to tighten around his neck like a python readying itself for dinner. He closed his eyes and spoke out loud, "I rebuke this spirit of control in the name of Jesus. Be gone!"

He took a deep breath as he pulled at his shirt collar, trying to loosen it. He felt better, at least for the moment.

Pastor Billings winced at the sound of the buzzer on his intercom. He prayed for strength.

"Pastor, Deacon Walters is here. He says he's only got fifteen minutes."

"That's fine. Send him in."

The pastor stood to his feet and consciously tried to smile as Dean walked into the room.

"Well, Pastor Billings, it's good to see you," announced the deacon in a deep, authoritative voice. "I assume you need my opinion on the upcoming building project?"

Evan glanced at the deacon and said, "Have a seat, Dean."

As usual, Dean tried to take charge of the situation. But before he could say more than a few words, Evan quickly interjected, "Dean, please give me the floor for a couple of minutes. This isn't about what you think."

The deacon didn't appreciate the pastor's tone...and it showed. He crossed his arms and glared at the pastor. He didn't appreciate the pastor's taking control.

"I've called this meeting not for your advice, but because the Holy Spirit has..." he paused. The intimidating look across the desk could have melted a glacier. "The Holy Spirit has ordered it."

Dean rolled his eyes and commented, "Why is it that you pastors always seem to think you have a corner on the Holy Spirit? But this is your meeting, so go ahead."

The spiritual warfare was intense, but a fresh touch of the Spirit invigorated Evan right when he needed it. Boldly, he spoke what was on his heart.

"I'm sure you would agree that it is very important for the deacons in this church to be biblically qualified."

Dean wasn't sure what to make of the pastor's words. Was he speaking about him as head of the deacons, or about somebody beneath him? He wasn't used to this confrontation, especially from the pastors who had served "under" him in the past thirty years.

Evan swallowed hard and continued, "We've worked very closely together over the past five years, Dean. It's obvious that God has blessed you with a great deal of talent, but it seems that you always need to receive credit for what you do. As your pastor, I felt a responsibility to talk with you about this issue."

Dean's face turned ghostlike; then bright, angry color flashed on his face. He didn't try to hide his outrage. He stood to his feet and walked deliberately around the desk. Evan didn't budge a muscle. He knew this wasn't going to be easy, but he had learned through the years that the most worthwhile blessings often came through life's darkest, loneliest moments. Evan's eyes widened as they looked up at Dean.

"I'm not trying to hurt your feelings, Dean. I really want to help you and your—"

Dean exploded, "Don't involve my family in this. We have our problems, but they aren't your business."

Evan tried to remain calm, but with a 250-pound tiger foaming in his face it wasn't easy.

"I have a responsibility before God to bring up this issue. You are our head deacon, and your actions represent this church to our members and this community."

Dean pointed his finger in Evan's face and growled, "Yes, let's talk about my job. I was doing it when you were in diapers. I've been at this church for a long time, and for you to insult me in this manner is ludicrous."

"I'm not trying to insult you. I'm trying to—"

"You're trying to assert your authority over me," interrupted Dean in a rage Evan had never seen. "This isn't about my pride. It's about your desire for power, and I can promise you, you won't get it!"

Without the Spirit's help, the pastor would have lost his temper and tried to defend himself from Dean's accusations. Instead, he spoke calmly.

"Dean, I know that we haven't always seen eye-to-eye on every matter. But I wish you wouldn't take this so personally. Don't you want to be more godly?"

You could see the veins popping out in Dean's forehead. He had been waiting for the right opportunity to tell this young buck what he really thought of him.

"More godly? I've been a Christian since long before you were born. I've seen four pastors come and go in my tenure here, and none of them had the gall to speak to me like this!"

Evan could have said, "None of them had the guts to stand up to you. Maybe you're the reason they left." But he didn't.

Dean continued in his rampage. "Because of me, this church is still here. I'm the reason half the people haven't left already. Your preaching is too hard. Your guilt trips from the pulpit are making people uncomfortable. You've got to stop talking about all of this holiness junk. And if I were you, I'd quit preaching about tithing. People are talking about you—and it's not good!"

Evan humbly replied, "I'm just preaching the Word the way I see it."

"Did you ever consider you may be wrong, preacher? Some of your literal translations of the Bible are driving people away from this church. And you're accusing *me* of being proud! Humph!" Dean pounded his fist on the pastor's desk. "I'm head deacon here. I have a God-given responsibility to run this church the way I see fit."

"What about God?" asked Evan.

"God?" retorted Dean. "God is on my side, and He knows I'm the most dedicated member in this church. You mind your business, pastor, and I'll take care of mine."

Dean stormed out of the office before Evan could respond. The sound of the slamming door was fresh in his ears as he pondered his next move. He knew Dean couldn't see his pride; it had clouded his vision. Evan dropped on his knees and prayed for God's help.

Religious pride is a special form of pride, tailor-made by the devil himself.

- Pride says, "I don't need God"; religious pride says, "God really needs me."
- Pride says, "Look at what I did! I'm something special"; religious pride says, "God, look at what I did! Wasn't it great?"
- Pride says, "Think of yourself. You are number one"; religious pride says, "Think of God. You are His number-one man."

When I was nine years old, my favorite pastime was building dams made of mud on the little stream that ran through our property. I would spend hours building a towering wall of mud several feet high, only to watch it eventually collapse under the weight of the building water. The most exciting part was trying to repair the walls before they collapsed. If I caught the leak soon enough, I could strengthen the dam and put off the inevitable—complete destruction. But, ultimately, the force of the water always won! Religious pride is like that water rising and building against the dam. You can't stop it without divine help.

Religious pride surfaced a long time ago. Adam and Eve were created perfect in every way, and their relationship with the Creator was strong and vibrant. Their consciences were clear; sin and pride were foreign to them. Beauty, paradise, and perfection were all they knew. They had never experienced temptation...until the devil slithered into the Garden.

Now the serpent was more crafty than any of the wild animals the LORD God had made. He said to the woman, "Did God really say, 'You must not eat from any tree in the garden'?" The woman said to the serpent, "We may eat fruit from the trees in the garden, but God did say, 'You must not eat fruit from the tree that is in the middle of the garden, and you must not

touch it, or you will die.'" "You will not surely die," the serpent said to the woman. "For God knows that when you eat of it your eyes will be opened, and you will be like God, knowing good and evil." (Gen. 3:1–5)

Where did the devil come from, and why was he bent on deceiving the first humans? We know the devil was created as a spirit or angel, and that he was perhaps the strongest of the angels by God's side. God cast Satan from heaven for sinning. What was his sin? The book of Isaiah relates the story.

How you have fallen from heaven, O morning star, son of the dawn! You have been cast down to the earth, you who once laid low the nations! You said in your heart, "I will ascend to heaven; I will raise my throne above the stars of God; I will sit enthroned on the mount of assembly, on the utmost heights of the sacred mountain. I will ascend above the tops of the clouds; I will make myself like the Most High." (Isa. 14:12–14)

The devil's sin was pride. And God's response was something like this: "Lucifer, I'm kicking you out of heaven. You are tempting and destroying My angels. You have said to yourself, 'I am as good as God, and it's about time people knew it!'"

This was probably the first instance of religious pride. It occurred with an angel named Lucifer. He may have been created as the most beautiful and possibly the most powerful of God's creatures, but he was no match for the Creator. For some reason not explained by the Bible, the devil turned on God. Instead of worshiping Him, he wanted to be like God; instead of loving God, he was jealous of Him; and instead of obeying God, he despised Him. Religious pride doesn't deny God's existence; rather, it distorts the image of God, His Word, and His ways. Religious pride has three primary components, all them evident in the Garden of Eden.

First, religious pride questions God's Word. The first words to Eve from the devil's mouth are cunning, deceitful, and deadly. He said, *"Did God really say, 'You must not eat from any tree in the garden'?"* (Gen. 3:1). Satan doesn't like the way God runs heaven or earth. Hence, he questions the orders of the Commander-in-Chief. In the military, it is an unconscionable offense to ignore the direct orders of a superior officer. The penalty for such willful pride and foolishness is swift and severe. Questioning orders can quickly result in a court-martial and time in the brig. Satan, in essence, questioned God's orders, His wisdom, and His authority to rule His creation.

Today, people from every walk of life question God's Word. The inerrancy of Scripture is hotly debated among those who should know better. The truths of the Bible are thrown aside by some in the church and are being replaced with man-made wisdom that originates from Satan's lying mouth. Religious pride says, "The Bible is a good book with good truths, but don't take it literally. Some of it is actually out-of-date, so live life the way that seems right to you."

Could you imagine trying to play the Super Bowl without a rule book? Every detail down to the color of the end zone grass is planned well in advance. Literally hundreds of rules are created for one purpose: for the game to run smoothly. Even devout football fans are unaware of dozens of rules and regulations for special circumstances that inevitably occur from time to time. The Bible is the Rule Book of life. A game without rules invites chaos and division. How's your knowledge of the Rule Book?

Second, religious pride twists, adds to, or subtracts from God's Word. When Eve responded to Satan, she did something very unusual for a sinless being. She added to the Word of God. God had told Adam, *"You are free to eat from any tree in the garden; but you must not eat from the tree of the knowledge of good and evil"* (Gen. 2:16–17). Yet Eve told the devil that they were not to eat from it—*or to touch it* (Gen. 3:3). Scripture does not record this command. I believe that Eve's distortion of God's original words caused the fruit of the tree to become even more desirable, thus heightening the urge to disobey.

Today, people from every denomination are making this same mistake. They add to the commandments and to the expectations that God has for His people, making it increasingly difficult to live a "proper" Christian life. In particular, legalistic Christians require those under them to obey so many man-made rules that God's truth gets buried underneath this religious burden. Jesus reminds us in Matthew 11:30, *"My yoke is easy and my burden is light."* Religious pride distorts the Bible, and the devil is behind all these shenanigans. He wants to turn the life-changing truths of the Word of God into watered-down teachings. He wants people to be confused over what is really God's truth. People consumed with religious pride cannot hear from God because the voice of God is not understandable to them. Jesus says in Matthew 11:15, *"He who has ears, let him hear."* Open your ears to God and His Word! Religious pride closes them, often permanently! Have you ever manually scrolled on your radio? A minor move to the left or right can often completely tune out the radio signal. Pride moves you far enough from God's frequency to make His voice unrecognizable.

Third, religious pride says you can be like God. Satan lied when he told Eve, "You will not surely die...for God knows that when you eat of it your eyes will be opened, and you will be like God, knowing good and evil" (Gen. 3:4–5). Religious pride allows a subtle but noxious form of evil to enter our lives and suffocate our souls. The proud love to flaunt their godliness and religious practices, yet their hearts are far from God. This form of pride also breeds a feeling of superiority. It looks down on those who don't agree with its rules and regulations.

Scripture is replete with examples of men and women of God who fell into the deadly trap of religious pride.

Remember the people who tried to build the Tower of Babel?

> *Then they said, "Come, let us build ourselves a city, with a tower that reaches to the heavens, so that we may make a name for ourselves and not be scattered over the face of the whole earth."*   (Gen. 11:4)

Why did they want to build such a high tower? Were they limited in space? Were they just having some fun? No, they wanted to erect a tower to get as close to God as possible. In short, they wanted to memorialize themselves. They wanted to *"make a name"* for themselves. Did they want to give glory to God? I don't think so. Pride had so consumed these people with visions of power that they undertook a huge building project to make their statement to the entire world. If an inscription had been written at the base of this monument, it probably would have read something like this: "This building is dedicated to God. We are His chosen people and His richest blessings have fallen on us. This tower is proof of His love for us and is evidence of our great wisdom and abilities."

These people did not want to be scattered across the earth. Their desire was directly against God's command to Noah and his sons: *"Be fruitful and increase in number and fill the earth"* (Gen. 9:1). These descendants of Noah didn't accept God's plan. Their pride led them to erect a huge monument in an effort to bring honor to themselves. Isn't it strange that in some people's attempt to please God, their religious pride often causes them to disobey Him?

David wrote out of his own experience with pride when he said, *"You save the humble but bring low those whose eyes are haughty"* (Ps. 18:27). As you read 2 Samuel 11:1–12:14, you can easily see David's pride as he seduced Bathsheba. Though God was greatly displeased with David, He forgave him because he repented of his adultery, murder, and pride.

Spiritual pride can make a sneak attack on even the most godly of individuals. One minute, you can be sailing into the sunset of God's glory without a care in the world. Your boat is steady as it effortlessly glides through life's waters. Your relationship with God is strong, your heart is humble and meek, and your salvation is secure. You sing, "All is well with my soul." Within minutes, you inadvertently doze off. Because you're asleep, you don't notice the storm clouds rising against the darkening horizon or the lightning cascading from the sky or the boat-sized waves approaching from the east. Suddenly, without warning, you awake to a tempest of enormous proportions. What happened? Where did it come from? You fell asleep on the job, and the devil came uninvited to turn your world upside down. Jesus warns us repeatedly through Scripture to be sober and alert. Mark 13:35–37 says,

> *Therefore keep watch because you do not know when the owner of the house will come back—whether in the evening, or at midnight, or when the rooster crows, or at dawn. If he comes suddenly, do not let him find you sleeping. What I say to you, I say to everyone: "Watch!"*

Jesus tells us to be strong in Him, be alert, watch for attacks from the enemy, and be ready for His second coming. Sadly, David had fallen asleep on the job. Years earlier, his love for God was phenomenal. God had chosen him to be the next king of Israel because his heart was like God's heart. He wanted the things of God more than land, money, power, or fame. But something changed. Scripture tells us, *"In the spring, at the time when kings go off to war, David sent Joab out with the king's men and the whole Israelite army"* (2 Sam. 11:1). Right there, Scripture give us a snapshot into David's heart. He had always led the men into war. He was the commander of the army. He was the king! But for some reason, this time, he didn't go. I believe religious pride was beginning to take hold of him. He was probably thinking something like this: *I don't need to go off and fight. Let someone else do it. I'm too important for that stuff. If I were to die, what would happen to my country?*

The rest of the story is simply a reflection of a heart filled with spiritual pride. David saw a beautiful woman bathing. Lust took control. He discovered she was married, but that didn't stop him. He called for her to come to him and sleep with him. His pride told him he could get away with it because he was so important. Hey, he had hundreds of wives already; one more conquest wasn't going to change God's opinion of him. His pride told him God wasn't watching that closely. His pride told him his past righteousness and purity were enough for God. His pride told him he could get away with murder because he was a man after God's own heart. (See Acts 13:22.)

King David fell asleep at the wheel of life, and the subsequent crash cost him dearly. He lost the respect of many around him; worse yet, he lost a son. Because of that one sin, there was strife, discord, chaos, backstabbing, and infighting in his family for generations to come. Yes, it was forgiven, but the consequences would remain. The price tag for religious pride is costly. David's example should warn all the family of Christ. "Don't go that way! The danger is great; the consequences are devastating!"

Pride does destructive things to God's family. Remember the story of Cain and Abel? (See Genesis 4:1– 7.) Abel took care of the flocks while his brother Cain worked the fields. When both brothers brought an offering to the Lord, Abel's was accepted, but God did not look with favor upon Cain's. Cain became *"very angry, and his face was downcast"* (v. 5). He felt that his offering should have received honor. After all, he had worked really hard on his sacrifice. God asked Cain why he was angry. He warned him that if he would *"do what is right"* (v. 7), he would be accepted; but if he allowed sin, which was *"crouching"* (v. 7) at his door, to become his master, it would prove to be his ruin. Rather than humbly seeking God's forgiveness, Cain allowed his pride to grow into jealousy and hatred, which led him to murder his own brother.

In the New Testament, we see many examples of people who were brought low because of their pride. Let's look for a moment at Peter. After spending nearly three years with Jesus, learning the deep truths of God, Peter fell for the ultimate trick of Satan. The scene opens with the disciples arguing over who would be considered the greatest of the apostles. These men didn't get it! Jesus was humble, a Servant sent to serve. He had modeled this lifestyle for them, yet they didn't catch on. Since Jesus singled out Peter in the verses that follow, perhaps he was the loudest and most boisterous of the group.

> *A dispute arose among them as to which of them was considered to be greatest. Jesus said to them, "The kings of the Gentiles lord it over them; and those who exercise authority over them call themselves Benefactors. But you are not to be like that. Instead, the greatest among you should be like the youngest, and the one who rules like the one who serves. For who is greater, the one who is at the table or the one who serves? Is it not the one who is at the table? But I am among you as one who serves."..."Simon, Simon, Satan has asked to sift you as wheat. But I have prayed for you, Simon, that your faith may not fail. And when you have turned back, strengthen your brothers." But he replied, "Lord, I am ready to go with you to prison and to death." Jesus answered, "I tell you, Peter, before the rooster crows today, you will deny three times that you know me."*
> (Luke 22:24–27, 31–34)

Can you imagine the way this dispute could have started?

"I left my entire family to follow the Lord!" one disciple bragged.

"I didn't even say good-bye to my father," added another.

"I didn't see any of you guys trying to walk on water!" Peter exclaimed.

Jesus shook His head in sadness. Religious pride was dividing them. The Lord said nothing as He continued to observe the sorry exchange.

"You didn't stay on top too long!" mocked one. "The wind and waves ate you alive! I saw you sink with my very own eyes."

Another disciple remarked, "I expect my mansion to be the largest. I'm the eldest among us, so I should receive the inheritance of the firstborn."

Peter couldn't help himself. He reminded them, "I was with Jesus, too, when Moses and Elijah appeared on the mountain. When the kingdom begins, I will be sitting next to Jesus on His throne."

What a picture of religious pride—arguing over who would be the greatest! Jesus quickly informed them they had everything backward. You would think that Peter would have been properly humbled when Jesus confronted their foolish bickering; instead, he declared that he was ready to go to jail for Christ or even to die for Him. Peter was the most zealous of the group, but he wasn't immune to the sin that desired to *"sift* [him] *as wheat."* Religious pride made Peter think more highly of himself than he should have. Romans 12:3 says,

> *For by the grace given me I say to every one of you: Do not think of yourself more highly than you ought, but rather think of yourself with sober judgment, in accordance with the measure of faith God has given you.*

The apostle Peter eventually learned this valuable lesson, but it came at a terrible price. He failed the Master he loved. What changed Peter into the man who courageously stood before the crowd in Jerusalem on the Day of Pentecost? What turned his pride into dependence on God? What enabled him to preach a message that brought about three thousand converts into the kingdom of God in one day? He was filled with the Holy Spirit. When the Spirit of God fills a person's heart, there is no room left for pride.

Jesus told a story about two brothers. In it, we can see a striking contrast between humble repentance and self-righteous pride. (See Luke 15:11–32.) The younger of the brothers asked his father for his inheritance. The boy took the money and ran. It wasn't long before he had squandered it all and found himself without any companions—except for the pigs he was hired to feed. In this sad state, he *"came to his senses"* (v. 17). He knew where he belonged...and he began the journey back home.

His father had not forgotten about him. Instead, he had been waiting, hoping, and praying for the return of his son. When he saw him coming, the father ran to him, *"threw his arms around him and kissed him"* (v. 20). In humility the son said, *"Father, I have sinned against heaven and against you. I am no longer worthy to be called your son"* (v. 21). The father's forgiveness was already given. He called for the servants to prepare a welcome-home celebration—complete with new clothes, shoes, a ring, and a delicious feast!

During the festivities, the older son returned home. Naturally, he wondered what was happening. One of the servants told him that his lost brother had come home and that their father was throwing a party to celebrate. Instead of reacting with joy, the older brother *"became angry and refused to go in"* (v. 28). Not even his father's pleadings could convince him to join the celebration. In contrast to his brother's admission, *"I have sinned,"* the older brother justified his reaction: *"'All these years I've been slaving for you and never disobeyed your orders'* (v. 29). What have all my good efforts brought me—nothing! Yet *'this son of yours'* (v. 30) [note his unwillingness to claim his lost brother] receives a grand welcome while my good works have been ignored."

Pride kept him from welcoming home his lost brother because pride built a barrier that kept love out. All these years he had lived in his father's house, but he hadn't take advantage of his privileges as a son. His father told him, *"You are always with me, and everything I have is yours"* (v. 31), but he had chosen to live in self-inflicted poverty, enclosed in a wall of selfish pride. Although he had not wandered far from home, he had wandered far from his father. Pride kept him from his father's embrace. Pride made him think of himself rather than his brother who had "come back to life."

What place does pride have in your life? Do you consider yourself to be a better person than most of those with whom you associate? Are you proud of all the time, money, and service you have invested in the kingdom? Do you think your church couldn't make it without you? Are you jealous when the service of others is applauded? Do you say to yourself, "I've done more than they have"? If so, you are bearing the pain and pride of the elder brother. The Father invites you to exchange your self-righteous rags for His robe of righteousness. Then you will be able to join in the celebration of the one who was lost but now is found.

Chapter Twelve

A Pastor's Confession

"For the Son of Man came to seek and to save what was lost."
—Luke 19:10

The following is the real-life story of a man who was lost in church. Although this is but one man's story, it is repeated continually throughout the world today.

Chuck leaned back in his chair, his hands clasped behind his head. His genuine smile hid all but a hint of nervous energy as he watched me power up my computer. Chuck has been an associate pastor for five years. He's in his late thirties and married with kids. He has been a Christian for over thirteen years, though most of his friends and acquaintances—including himself for a time—thought he had been a Christian his entire life. A flurry of emotions surface as I ask him about his past.

Q: "Do you remember much about church growing up?"

A: "When I was seven or eight years old, we were the 'C' and 'E' Christians. We showed up for Christmas and Easter. My parents called themselves Christians, but now I know they were lost." The pain in Chuck's voice is obvious. "I don't remember going to one church. We would go to this one, then that one. They would pick and choose as time went along."

Q: "Did you eventually settle on a church home?"

A: "We did after we moved to the country. From fourth grade through my teenage years, we attended the same church."

Q: "What did you learn about God in that church?"

A: "I honestly don't remember learning much of anything." Chuck looks frustrated as he remembers the effect this dead church had on him and his family. This church, its pastor and leadership, and its members had a God-given duty to spread the Gospel; instead, they were a social organization with rigid rules and rampant hypocrisy. "Nothing really stuck with me. We didn't talk about drugs or alcohol being wrong or practically anything else that I can remember." He shakes his head in disbelief.

Q: "What kind of example did your dad set for you?"

A: "He was lost just like the rest of us and doing what he had been taught." Chuck quickly adds, "My dad was a very moral person. There was no cursing, no alcohol in our home. We were a clean-cut family. Dad was the big 'truth, justice, and the American way' kind of guy. I thought my dad was Superman." Chuck laughs as he thinks back. "He even looked like Superman. He was a straight-laced guy," he chuckles. "He was a high school assistant principal. He was very old-fashioned."

Q: "Do you remember him talking to you about God?"

A: "Not really. He was a Sunday school teacher for the youth, then for the married adults, but he didn't have a real relationship with the Lord. He was a naturally gifted teacher, but he didn't have the Holy Spirit."

Q: "Did he ever talk to you about being born again?"

A: "No. His attitude was, 'I've done my part by sending you to church.' He never had a real conversation with me about being born again. I honestly don't think he even understood what that term meant. Our church didn't teach that stuff. I do remember the time he talked to me about sex. He went through all the mechanical parts of it but never discussed the spiritual side of it. He did say it was what married people did, but that's it. He never went into the 'why' part."

Q: "What else do you remember about your dad?"

A: "I remember one time..." Chuck grimaces and shifts in his seat. "I called a young man the 'N' word, and I got the beating of my life. I never did that again...ever! Dad was a very moral man."

Note: Chuck tells me his father is still lost and in need of a Savior. He still attends church, but it's extremely liberal and seldom addresses topics of sin or salvation. Chuck's witnessing has fallen on deaf ears. It's a tragedy reflected in the pain on Chuck's face when he talks about his dad.

Q: "How about your mom? What was she like, and what kind of influence did she have on you as it pertains to God?"

A: "She was a very firm woman, an intellectual woman who was very honest with her feelings and her struggles. She didn't believe things just because she was supposed to or because somebody else did. Church was Dad's thing, but she figured it was good to connect with society because of Dad's job. Dad thought church was a good way to get to know people." He stops to gather his thoughts. "I'm not trying to cast a bad light on Dad, but I'm sure that's one of the reasons we were in church every Sunday. Mom was basically an agnostic. Church and God didn't really connect with her, but she didn't allow that to affect our decisions either. She never talked to me about God."

Q: "How about their relationship? Was it a godly one?"

A: "They had a really good relationship. It was an old-fashioned marriage with him making the financial decisions. He did what he was good at, and she did what she was good at. It was a very functional family, and we had lots of fun together. I have two younger sisters, and we bought a house way out in the boondocks and renovated it." Chuck's eyes brighten at the memory.

Note: Chuck grew up in a very good family in a time when traditional families were the norm and not the exception. Church, family, and country were priorities for them; they were good people, church people, yet lost people. There was no abuse or addictions or anything else that would normally drive people away from God; they were a strong unit who did all the right things, yet they didn't have a personal relationship with the Savior. Unfortunately, this same story is being played out all over the world today.

Q: "Did you think of yourselves as a godly family?"

A: "It never even crossed my mind back then."

Q: "Tell me about your teenage years. Were they tumultuous like so many others?"

A: "I did some bad stuff...the normal bad stuff that many teenagers did in the 70s. My biggest weakness was with alcohol and the ladies."

Q: "Did you ever ask yourself what God thought of what you were doing?"

A: "Oh, no. I never thought about God. I was worried about Dad finding out. I was concerned about his reputation as a high school assistant principal and what he might do to me."

Q: "Didn't you learn about sin in church?"

A: "I remember nothing—nothing that sticks with me. Maybe we talked about it, but it certainly didn't affect me. I'm just not sure. I knew I was doing wrong, but I didn't know why."

Note: Chuck's God-given conscience was working, but the Holy Spirit wasn't molding it. Instead, he was guided more by social traditions and morals.

Q: "If somebody had asked you if you were a Christian, what would you have said?"

A: "Before I was sixteen, I would have said yes and pointed to the church I was going to then. But, at sixteen, I remember being up very late one night and listening to a televangelist. He invited people to say the prayer of salvation...and I did. A number flashed on the screen for people to call, but when I tried to call, it was busy. I was mad that I couldn't get through. It was a very emotional time." Chuck's tone was somber and reflective.

Q: "So you got saved that night?"

A: The look on Chuck's face turns serious, yet sad. "No, but at the time, I thought I had."

Q: "What do you mean? You said that prayer, didn't you?"

A: "Yes, I did, but it's obvious I didn't mean it."

Q: "How do you know you didn't?"

A: "Well, I thought about it for a day or two but didn't think about it again. There was absolutely no change in my life."

Q: "No fruit at all?"

A: "I went back to business as usual—partying it up, messing with the ladies, drinking more than I should have, and all the time thinking that I was now on my way to heaven."

Q: "When did you think about God again?"

A: "The next year, when I was seventeen, I met Tonya, my future wife. She was only fourteen at the time."

Q: "Her dad let you date her?"

A: "Yes, but only if I went to their church. I wanted to date her, so I went to their church. She was pretty; it was a very easy decision. It was very different from the churches I had attended before."

Q: "How was it different?"

A: "I heard things that I'd never heard at my parents' church. It really got me thinking about things. They taught the entire Bible, something my parents' church didn't do."

Q: "Didn't they ask you if you were saved? It sounds like you were going to a Bible-believing church."

A: "Her mother was very bold, and she did ask me. I told her that I got saved last year."

Q: "Did she accept that?"

A: "Yes, she did. They saw me as a very moral young man. They didn't see the other side of me. Why would she question it?"

Note: Chuck's story is sobering. He wasn't saved and everybody—including himself at this time—thought he was born again. Even if people examined his life closely for spiritual fruit, they may very well have come away believing the lie. He hid his sin well, even from himself. Satan is masterful in this area. The Holy Spirit is the only power that can open the eyes of somebody so deceived.

Q: "I assume Tonya was a Christian at this time?"

A: "Oh, yes. She's been a Christian since she was seven years old. She was by far the most moral and godly girl I had ever met."

Q: "Did she suspect anything?"

A: "I don't think so. She acted just like her mother. She asked me once, and I told her what I had told her mother. It was as if she wanted me to be a Christian. It's like I was applying for a job. It was just another check in the box. What's your sex? What's your hair color? What's your social security number? And, oh, by the way, are you a Christian? It was taken at face value. I made it easy for them to believe the lie. I did all the right things at the right times." Chuck pauses as he reflects on what was happening at that time. "I think part of it was the status thing. My dad was a high school assistant principal. I was on the basketball team. I think that affected their judgments some. It makes people think things about you that aren't really true. They want to believe the best without finding out the truth."

Q: "What would happen at church?"

A: "The sermons would definitely get me thinking. I felt something, but I wasn't sure what it was. I understood true Christianity a lot more clearly. I learned more about sin and salvation and personal responsibility and that it was a personal relationship. They would give altar calls, which is something they never did at my parents' church. I never thought I needed to go—hey, I'd been there, done that. I said that prayer. What more did I need to do?"

Q: "Was Tonya ever suspicious that you weren't a Christian?"

A: "Not really. I mean, she didn't like my friends too much, so I hid my friendships and the alcohol from her. No need for her to know about my buddies or the booze. Didn't want to hurt her or lose her."

Q: "What happened after graduation?"

A: "Well, she had three more years of high school, so I enlisted in the Army. We had a long-distance relationship for those years."

Q: "What happened with God?"

A: "I grew farther away from Him. I was plenty immoral and I was becoming increasingly lonely. And then that's when I got baptized."

Q: "Baptized? How in the world did that happen? I thought you were straying farther from God."

A: "I was in Florida after boot camp, and a bunch of us guys were invited to this church for a revival. We decided to go. The message was hard-hitting, and I was convicted in a big way. They talked a lot about being baptized."

Q: "Why did you do that?"

A: "I thought it was the right thing to do. I figured I was already saved, and I needed to follow it up with baptism."

Q: "So you were baptized, but you weren't saved?"

A: "Yep. No one had ever asked me if I had been baptized, and that church service really did a number on me."

Q: "Did you have even an inkling that you weren't saved?"

A: "Not really. I figured I was. I had said that prayer, and now I was baptized. What more did God want from me? I was in church all the time and did the right things most of the time. I was totally fooled in every way possible, and everybody around me bought it."

Q: "You were married a few years later?"

A: "We married when Tonya graduated from high school. She was eighteen, and I was twenty-one. We moved to the city. I'll never forget the first day we woke up in our new home. We went out, ate breakfast, then found a church. I was following in my father's footsteps. He almost always did the right thing, and I wanted to do the same. I was recreating my dad's life step-by-step."

Q: "Did Tonya suspect anything after the marriage? Was your marriage going well...in a spiritual sense?"

A: "Absolutely. She didn't suspect a thing, nor did I. She took everything at face value. She never doubted my salvation. We were high school sweethearts; we were newlyweds. Everything was great."

Q: "Tell me about this church. Was it like your dad's church?"

A: "No way." Chuck smiles. "They preached it the way it was. It was a little country church in the middle of the big city. They were simple, plain people who loved us. There were seventy-five, maybe eighty people. We were at home in the middle of the city."

Q: "Did they ask you about your walk with God?"

A: "They asked if we were saved and baptized." Chuck shrugged. "I told them yes and yes on both counts. What else were they supposed to ask? In a way, they wanted me to be saved. They were good folks, simple, nice, kind. It was easy to be around them...to fit in. It was a close-knit atmosphere. On Sunday nights lots of people would hang out in the church parking lot after services and talk for hours. They were like family."

Q: "And they asked you to be a deacon?"

A: "You bet. We were in church whenever the doors were open. I was very committed to the church and fit all the biblical qualifications for a deacon."

Q: "Except...?"

A: "Well..." Chuck shakes his head and sighs. "I wasn't a Christian, and I started to realize it little by little. Don't get me wrong. At the time, I thought I was a Christian. My in-laws came, and I'll never forget how happy Tonya's father was for me. I was the youngest deacon the church has ever had." Chuck's face droops. "It was quite an accomplishment."

Q: "How long did it take for you to start feeling conviction?"

A: "It was at the birth of our first child, Nicole. I'll never forget watching the birth, and I started thinking about the circle of life. It was like...this is my child, the next generation. I'm totally responsible for her. I suddenly saw my own mortality through the birth of our child, and it scared me." Chuck grips the edge of his desk with a tight hold. "I started to wake up in the middle of the night, and I was scared to death. I started thinking about death and dying, and it scared me...a lot. I've always been a sound sleeper, but I started waking up in a cold sweat." Chuck stares at the wall. "It really started getting to me."

Q: "How long did this continue?"

A: "About two years." Chuck exhales loudly. Thoughts about his past are getting to him. "I would sit in church and listen to the pastor preach...and, boy, could he preach! It used to be I was convinced of my salvation, but as time went by, I began to feel guilt...to feel an emptiness that wouldn't go away. I was becoming miserable. The preaching was relentless, and the conviction just got worse and worse. Obviously, the Holy Spirit was chipping away at me."

Q: "Why didn't you settle the matter and give it up?"

A: Chuck tips his head and smiles. "I was a deacon, and for a while, I still thought, or at least hoped, I was saved." He pauses, reliving the conflict of those days. "I couldn't walk the aisle. Deacons don't go forward to get saved. What would people think? He's a phony, fake, liar, pretender. I was scared to death. Maybe I was saved and the devil was playing tricks with me. Then I thought, no way. I know I'm not."

Q: "Was there any joy in your life at this time?"

A: "There was some. I was a new father and had a great wife. That kept me going. I would try to forget about it, but every church service would remind me again. The pounding from God was getting worse and worse, but I would shake it off the following day."

Q: "How about Tonya? Didn't she think something was up?"

A: Chuck thinks for a moment. "She knew there was something wrong but didn't know how to help. She figured I was saved, baptized, a deacon; it couldn't be spiritual. I didn't tell her the truth about my salvation; I still wasn't sure myself." He pauses as he looks at the floor. "I couldn't." Chuck's voice is low and trembling. "I started feeling hollow inside. I was getting depressed, but I didn't show it on the outside. I hid it well. Within a year I knew for sure I wasn't saved. Then I started feeling like a major hypocrite. Look, I'm a very logical person, so I started to examine my life and say, 'What's happening here? I'm not acting like a Christian. A Christian doesn't do the things I do.' I struggled with lots of guilt and shame. And then...the fight was really on."

Q: "So you didn't rush to the altar and get it taken care of?"

A: "No. I would listen to the sermons, and they would cut me apart, but I kept asking myself, 'What will people think of me? Are you sure you're not saved?' I couldn't confess like that and run to the front of the church. People wouldn't understand. I thought it would be a disaster."

Note: The lies from the enemy only increase as the Holy Spirit faithfully convicts a person. The devil senses he is losing control and will do anything in his power to deceive the lost. One of the greatest lies he perpetuates is convincing lost people that they are already saved.

Q: "Did you talk to anybody about it?"

A: "I said something to a few friends in church. I told them I was having doubts—that I wasn't sure if I was a Christian." Chuck shakes his head. "They all told me the same thing: I was fine. I had said the sinner's prayer, and I meant it. I'd been baptized. I was a deacon! What was the problem? It couldn't be my salvation. Maybe the devil was playing tricks on me."

Q: "Why do you think they reacted like that?"

A: Chuck appears confident in his reply. "I don't think they wanted *their* world shaken. If I wasn't a Christian with everything I'd done, then who was? Maybe they were going through the same stuff but had ignored it as an attack by the devil. If they really dug deep, maybe they would need to reexamine their lives. I don't think they wanted to do that." Chuck quotes Matthew 5:20: *"For I tell you that unless your righteousness surpasses that of the Pharisees and the teachers of the law, you will certainly not enter the kingdom of heaven."* He sighs heavily. "Deacons who aren't saved. Preachers who aren't saved. That's some scary stuff!"

Q: "So how did you get saved?"

The following is the account of that memorable day, July 10, 1988.

A low, hanging fog was draped across the slowly brightening sky as Chuck and his family drove to church. It was Sunday, and like every other Sunday for the past several years, they were faithfully attending their small country church in the midst of the city.

"Is everything okay?" asked Tonya, a bit concerned by Chuck's silence.

Chuck didn't respond. His mind was in another world.

"Chuck!" Tonya called.

"Huh?" He glanced at her as he turned the car into the parking lot.

"What's up with you? You've been awfully quiet lately. Are you mad at me?"

Chuck grabbed her hand. "I'm sorry, honey. I've just got a lot of things on my mind lately. I'll be fine."

His smile reassured her. "If you need to talk," she squeezed his hand, "I'm here."

Chuck nodded. He was distracted again, and she knew it. She was trying to be a good Christian wife, but she felt powerless over this invisible force vying for his attention. Several minutes later, they were seated in the middle of the small sanctuary, listening to the pastor preach his heart out.

"You must be born again to be saved!" preached Pastor Barnes.

Chuck leaned forward in his seat.

"No amount of religion or good works will get you to heaven!"

Chuck placed his hands on the pew in front of him.

"Too many people are playing church, going through all the motions, doing all the right things, nodding their heads at the right times to what the preacher says." He paused and looked out at the people. "And they're as lost as the drug addict on the corner!"

Chuck gripped the pew and squeezed until his knuckles turned white. The words were ripping him apart. He couldn't stand it anymore. He was tired of living a lie, tired of waking up at night in cold sweats, tired of wondering if he would be flattened by a semi-truck and sent straight to hell.

"If you are lost and sitting in church, God will be angrier at you on Judgment Day than with those who never showed up for church." The pastor's expression couldn't have been more serious. "Jesus died a horrible death to free you from your sins."

Chuck's hands began to quiver against the assault from heaven. The noise in his head was unbearable. His eyes turned blurry as the barrage from God intensified.

Pastor Barnes appeared to look directly at Chuck. Chuck's heart leaped in his chest. Did the pastor know? How could he? Chuck swallowed and closed his eyes. He felt hopeless. He knew he couldn't do it. The mere thought of walking to the front of the church made him sick.

"God cannot be fooled. You can fool me, you can fool your spouse, you can fool your kids, and you can fool your neighbors." His voice grew louder. "But God Almighty cannot be mocked! Every knee will bow and every tongue will confess that Jesus Christ is Lord."

Chuck glanced nervously at his wife. She was staring at the preacher, completely enthralled by the message. She didn't see his tears, his heart, his soul, longing to break free from the lies that chained him to doubt, pain, and depression.

"Please bow your head," asked the preacher as the pianist quietly played a hymn.

"If you want Jesus Christ to come into your heart and cleanse you from all your sin, come down this aisle and meet me at the altar."

Preacher Barnes came off the platform and stood in front of the congregation. He stared at the people, praying that God would break their hearts. Chuck clutched onto Tonya's hand as they sang the hymn. She had no idea of the battle raging inside him, consuming him like a wildfire set loose in a dry forest. Chuck's feet didn't move. His heart was holding him back against his better judgment and against God's calling. He was too embarrassed to make the right decision. Too many people would need an explanation. He could see it now...

Chuck slowly rounded the corner of the pew and made his way toward the front of the church, his head hanging low. With each step he took, row after row of people opened their eyes and stared at him in disbelief.

Pastor Barnes stared at him with shock. "What are you doing up here, Chuck?"

Chuck took a gulp of air and tried to speak. "I need to get saved."

"What did you say?" asked the pastor, shocked by what he thought he'd heard.

In a louder voice, Chuck announced so all could hear, "I need to get saved."

Pastor Barnes' face turned angry. "What do you mean you need to get saved?" Every eye was on Chuck. Shock filled the sanctuary. "You're a deacon in this church." The pastor's thunderous voice seemed to shake the rafters. "Why didn't you tell us you weren't saved before we made you a deacon?"

Chuck's knees shook as he tried to speak. "I...I don't know."

"You don't know? You do know! You are a fake, a fraud." The accusations rang in Chuck's head.

Suddenly, Tonya squeezed his hand.

"Are you okay, honey? You're sweating."

Chuck looked at her, then jerked his head to the left and the right. It had all been a nightmare!

"I'm...I'm fine," he stuttered, unbuttoning the top button on his collar.

Tonya closed her eyes and prayed. "Lord Jesus, please help Chuck. Touch him, and free him from whatever is binding him."

The Holy Spirit was at work in Chuck's heart. As the pastor closed the service, Chuck's resolve grew firm.

"I've got to talk to the pastor," he told his wife. "I'll meet you in the parking lot."

"Okay, honey," she told him with a smile.

Chuck made his way to the front of the church. He was glad that the people talking with the pastor were starting to leave.

"Pastor Barnes, could we speak in your office?"

"Sure, Chuck. What's up?"

Chuck didn't answer until they reached the pastor's office. He followed the pastor in and closed the door.

"Is there something wrong?"

Chuck stared at the pastor for a moment. The look on his face made Pastor Barnes uneasy.

"I don't want you to tell me I'm crazy or being emotional," began Chuck. "I don't want you saying to me that this isn't necessary."

Pastor Barnes looked at him without saying a word. He didn't know what to say. He just nodded.

Chuck paced back and forth in front of the pastor. Perspiration rolled down his face as he said, "I'm not a Christian...and don't tell me I am. I thought I was at one time, but I'm sure I'm not. I need to get saved, and I need to do it right now!"

For a moment, there was some shock on the pastor's face. That quickly disappeared. The pastor's voice was supportive and nonjudgmental. "Okay, Chuck." He opened his Bible and turned to John 3:16. "The Bible says, *'For God so loved the world that he gave his one and only Son, that whoever believes in him shall not perish but have everlasting life.'*"

He looked at Chuck. Chuck stood in front of him...staring at him almost mechanically. Pastor Barnes turned to another verse.

"The Bible also says in Romans 10:13, 'Everyone who calls on the name of the Lord will be saved.'"

Chuck nodded his head as tears accumulated in his eyes.

"Do you want to pray and ask Jesus to come into your heart and to live in you and change you? You need to mean it, Chuck." The pastor's words were straightforward.

Chuck was finished fighting God. Living a lie had been eating him alive. With joy and relief, he prayed.

"Lord Jesus, I'm sorry for my false faith. Forgive me, and fill me with Your Spirit. I invite You into my life to live with me. Amen."

Q: "Did you feel different after that prayer?"

A: "I didn't feel different at all. I mean, I didn't get real emotional or anything. I know some people feel that, but I didn't." Chuck places his hand on his Bible. "What I did know is that my eternity was sealed. The burden of guilt was lifted. The doubts and fears were gone."

Q: "How about those dreams and the nighttime spells?"

A: "Gone." He smiles.

Q: "How did Tonya react?"

A: "Well, she was waiting for me in the car. I looked her straight in the eyes and told her I had just gotten saved and that she knew better than anybody else I needed to do this. She completely accepted what I said; she wasn't judgmental or anything. She didn't appear too surprised. She knew it was a good thing and that the past was the past. At that moment, I realized I had deceived her all those years. I'll never forget that feeling. It ripped me apart inside."

Q: "Since your salvation, tell me what the difference has been in your life."

A: "There's been a slow but steady change through the years. I'm really growing closer to God. The fears and doubts are gone. There's a new awareness of Christ that doesn't go away when I leave the confines of the church." Chuck takes a deep breath. The look on his face speaks for his heart. All is well with his soul. "And my relationship with Tonya is even better now."

Q: "You've been a pastor for nearly five years. If people are struggling with their salvation, what would you tell them?"

A: "Ask yourself these questions: 'Do I have a real relationship with the Lord? Am I growing closer to Him and walking in obedience to His Word? Is there fruit in my life?' If you have fears and doubts, ask God if you are truly saved. He will let you know."

Q: "Do you question your salvation now?"

A: "No!"

Q: "Do you fear death?"

A: "No!"

Q: "Do you sense the Holy Sprit in your life?"

A: "Most of the time...yes." He chuckles. "Everybody has a bad day once in a while."

Q: "Why do you think you went through this?"

A: "I can help those who are going through the same struggles. And there are a lot of people in the church as lost as I was. The following Sunday after my conversion the pastor asked me to give my testimony to the whole church."

Q: "Were you excited about it?"

A: "Are you kidding? No! I was scared to death, but I knew it was the right thing to do. After I gave my testimony, two or three people came up to give their lives to Christ. They were lost and scared to death, too, but my obedience gave them the courage to settle things with God." Chuck's eyes fill with tears. "I'm just glad He saved me from that life. Being lost in church is in many ways worse than not being there at all. And all those fears of rejection were lies from the enemy. Everybody supported me at the church. Not one person condemned me."

Think about the implications of Chuck's story. How many people attending church today do not have a real relationship with the Lord? How many are trusting in their good works, their moral lifestyles, or their family upbringing to get them to heaven? How many are afraid to admit that they really don't know if they are saved? How many hold back from making a commitment to Christ because they are fearful of what others will think?

The Good News is that the Father continues to relentlessly pursue the lost—even the lost in church. It was to the scribes and Pharisees that Jesus told this story:

Suppose one of you has a hundred sheep and loses one of them. Does he not leave the ninety-nine in the open country and go after the lost sheep until he finds

it? And when he finds it, he joyfully puts it on his shoulders and goes home. Then he calls his friends and neighbors together and says, "Rejoice with me; I have found my lost sheep." (Luke 15:4–6)

Chuck was a lost sheep, yet Jesus relentlessly searched for him when other shepherds would have given up. Jesus cherishes and seeks all His lost sheep. His Word says, *"The Lord is...not willing that any should perish but that all should come to repentance"* (2 Peter 3:9 NKJV).

If you are a lost sheep today or one who has been straying outside—or inside—the safety of the fold, listen to the Good Shepherd's voice. He is calling you to follow Him...to obey Him...to be transformed by Him. Hear His Good News: You never have to be lost again.

About the Author

J onathan Cash is the author of two popular books, *The Age of the Antichrist* and *Thunder in Paradise,* both end-time thrillers about the last days of planet Earth. He is the meteorologist for one of the highest rated television morning shows in the country. Jonathan is also a sought-after evangelist and popular speaker. He resides in Chesapeake, Virginia, with his wife Tina and two children.

His passion for God and His Word has driven him to write *Lost in Church.* Jonathan believes the harvest field isn't just outside the church walls, but within them. He mixes real-life examples, fictional stories, parody, and sound, honest, easy-to-understand biblical teaching to get his message across.

ANOTHER POWERFUL Book
from Whitaker House

The Age of the Antichrist

Jonathan R. Cash

Hail mixed with blood rifles the earth; raging fires consume a third of the planet; locusts sting with the force of scorpions, torturing their victims; millions have disappeared, and yet the end is not here. One man is intent on holding the power of the universe in his hands. Can anything stop this man who would be god?

ISBN: 0-88368-629-5 • Trade • 400 pages

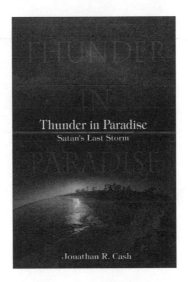

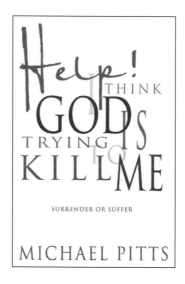

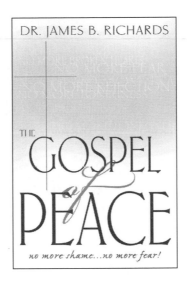

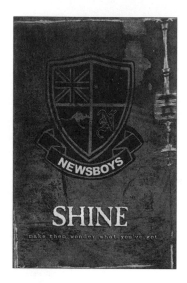